P9-DOH-890

THE ANIMAL MATING GAME

THE WACKY, WEIRD WORLD OF SEX IN THE ANIMAL KINGDOM

BY ANN DOWNER

TFCB

TWENTY-FIRST CENTURY BOOKS / MINNEAPOLIS

Twenty-First Century Books
A division of Lerner Publishing Group, Inc.
241 First Avenue North
Minneapolis, MN 55401 USA

For reading levels and more information, look up this title at www.lernerbooks.com.

Main body text set in Adrianna Regular 11/15.
Typeface provided by Chank.

Library of Congress Cataloging-in-Publication Data

Names: Downer, Ann, 1960– author.
Title: The animal mating game : the wacky, weird world of sex in the animal kingdom / by Ann
    Downer.
Description: Minneapolis : Twenty-First Century Books, [2016] | Audience: Grades 9–12. |
    Summary: "This book discusses courtship, sex, and mating habits across the animal kingdom,
    covering birds, reptiles, amphibians, fishes, and mammals, as well as select invertebrates."—
    Provided by publisher. | Includes bibliographical references and index.
Identifiers: LCCN 2015035704| ISBN 9781467785716 (lb : alk. paper) | ISBN 9781512411430
    (eb pdf : alk. paper)
Subjects: LCSH: Courtship in animals—Juvenile literature. | Sexual behavior in animals—Juvenile
    literature. | Sexual selection in animals—Juvenile literature.
Classification: LCC QL761 .D69 2016 | DDC 591.56—dc23

LC record available at http://lccn.loc.gov/2015035704

Manufactured in the United States of America
1-37923-19278-3/18/2016

CONTENTS

The male peacock is famous for his brilliant train of feathers, which he fans out to attract potential mates. Since female peacocks do not have to impress males, they have dull colors and no train of feathers.

INTRODUCTION: THE BIRDS AND THE BEES

When parents sit down to talk to their children about sex, they sometimes say, "It's time for you to learn about the birds and the bees." The origins of this phrase are unclear, but it means that sex isn't something that just people do. Almost every kind of animal mates, or has sex.

And along with mating comes dating. Just like human courtship, carried out to attract and impress potential mates, animal courtship involves showing off, gift giving, and affectionate gestures. Like some humans, some animals will fight one another to win a mate. Others will cheat on their lifelong partners. In the human world, it's not uncommon for an individual to have more than one sexual partner, and that's true in the animal world too. And as with human mating, animal sex doesn't always involve males coupling with females. Same-sex romantic partners also couple up in the animal world.

The mechanics of animal sex are often similar to the human sex act. The genitalia of the male and female partners fit together, one inside the other, enabling the male's sex cells (called sperm) to fertilize the female's sex cells (called eggs). But that's not always the case. Some animals, such as many types of fish, never touch one another when they mate. Other animals are hermaphrodites—they have both male and female sexual organs. With this equipment, these animals can mate with any other member of the same species, or type.

LOOKING FOR MR. RIGHT

In the animal world, it is usually the female that picks her mate. So male animals often work hard to impress females, offering fancy dance moves, beautiful songs, and spectacular looks. In many animal species, because the females don't have to impress the males, the females are drab while the males are colorful. (At the same time, drab coloring can help camouflage females, keeping them and their newborns safe from predators.)

When animals reproduce, each parent passes on genes to the offspring. Genes are made of a chemical called deoxyribonucleic acid (DNA), and they determine how an organism will look and behave. In most species, half the genes come from the father and half come from the mother, which is why offspring resemble their parents. When a female animal picks a mating partner, she is partly picking the characteristics she will pass on to her young. For example, if a female bighorn sheep chooses to mate with the biggest, strongest ram in the herd, she is doing her best to ensure that her offspring will also be big and strong—and therefore will be most likely to survive.

Choosing one male over another isn't necessarily a conscious choice on the part of a female animal. Most animals act on instinct—an inner knowledge that directs behavior. Animals do not have to learn instinctive behavior. They are born with this knowledge, which guides them in everything from building nests to choosing mates to raising their young.

BRINGING UP BABY

A few kinds of animals can reproduce asexually, without mating to merge egg and sperm. These animals include some kinds of flatworms, which sometimes reproduce by splitting into two pieces. The tail portion then grows a new head, and the head section grows a new tail—forming two flatworms from one. Some species of sea anemones grow small buds that eventually break off and become separate animals. But most animals reproduce sexually, with sperm from the male fertilizing eggs from the female. Fertilization can happen either outside or inside the female's body.

External fertilization is common among aquatic (water-dwelling) animals. These animals, such as many kinds of fish, release millions of eggs into the water. Then, without necessarily touching the females, males release their sperm into the water. The sperm swim to the eggs and fertilize them. Once fertilized, the eggs develop into offspring.

Internal fertilization occurs when eggs are fertilized inside the female's body during or after sex. Physical contact between the genitalia of the male and female allows sperm to meet and fertilize an egg (or eggs, depending on the type of animal). Among mammals, such as elephants, rabbits, dogs, and humans, the fertilized egg (or eggs) grows inside the female, and she eventually gives birth to a baby. Mammals raise their babies until they become independent. Sometimes, both parents care for the young, but usually just the mother does the job.

Bird reproduction is different. After her egg is fertilized during sex, a female bird will lay the egg, or force it out of her body. Inside each laid egg, a bird embryo (an unborn or unhatched offspring) begins to grow. For the developing bird to survive, the egg must be incubated, or kept warm. Sometimes just the mother bird keeps her eggs warm by sitting on them, warming them with her body heat. Sometimes just the father bird incubates the eggs, and sometimes both parents take turns. Once an embryo has developed into a chick, it breaks out of its shell. Bird parents care for newborn chicks until they are able to see, stand, fly, and find food on their own. (Farmers breed some birds, such as chickens, to lay unfertilized eggs, which people eat for food.)

Among amphibians (including frogs, toads, and salamanders) and reptiles (including alligators, lizards, and snakes), males and females mate, and the females lay fertilized eggs. But most amphibians and reptiles do not parent their young. The fathers usually leave

Among orangutans, mothers do all the child care. This mother and baby reside in a national park in Indonesia.

the mothers right after mating, and mothers usually lay their eggs and move on. The babies hatch alone and take care of themselves from the start. Arthropods, such as insects, spiders, lobsters, and crabs, are a mixed bag. Some female arthropods lay their eggs and leave before the babies hatch. Others stay with their eggs until they hatch.

Within all these animal groups are variations. For instance, external fertilization is common among fish, but sharks are different. Their eggs are fertilized internally through sexual intercourse. Among some shark species, mothers lay fertilized eggs in warm, shallow waters, where the embryos develop and then hatch. In other shark species, the embryos remain inside the mother, and she gives birth to live babies. Among seahorses, another kind of fish, the female lays unfertilized eggs inside a pouch in the male's body. He releases sperm to fertilize the eggs and carries the eggs until they are ready to hatch.

THE LIFE FORCE

The looks, behaviors, and anatomy of animal species sometimes change from generation to generation. Some changes begin with a mutation, or alteration, in an animal's genetic material. The animal passes this genetic mutation to its offspring. Some mutations are harmful and lead to disease. But some mutations help animals survive. For instance, a mutation might cause a change in an animal's coloration, from vibrant to dull. This dull coloration might allow the animal to better hide from predators. That gives it a better chance of surviving and eventually having offspring. The animal will pass on this advantageous coloration to its offspring through its DNA. Meanwhile, animals of the same species that still have bright coloration will be more vulnerable to predators and will be less likely to survive, produce offspring, and pass on their DNA. After many generations, the animals in the species with the bright coloration will have died out, and all animals of the species will have the dull coloration. This is called natural selection, or survival of the fittest.

In the nineteenth century, English naturalist Charles Darwin was the first scientist to describe natural selection. He noted how organisms that are best suited to their environment are most likely to survive and have offspring. Darwin also explained how mutations and natural selection, over many generations, could lead to the formation of entirely new species, which would be biologically distinct from their ancestors. Darwin proposed that life on Earth began with a single kind of organism that evolved, or changed gradually over the generations, into many new species. These species in turn evolved into more species, with plant and animal life eventually branching out to create the millions of species alive on Earth. Some religious groups have challenged the theory of evolution, but almost all twenty-first-century scientists agree with it. They say that the variety of plant and animal life on Earth has resulted from the intertwined processes of mutation, natural selection, and evolution.

END OF THE LINE

Survival isn't a given in the animal world. Since life on Earth began more than 3.5 billion years ago, millions of plant and animal species have gone extinct, or died out completely. Environmental changes—such as when a normally wet area becomes dry or when a normally cold area warms up—can cause extinction. Then the changing climate kills the plants or other animals that a certain animal species relies on for food, leading to the death of the species. Sometimes new animal species move into an area and prey on species that have previously lived there with few or no predators. The new predators drive the prey into extinction. Some extinctions are more dramatic. For instance, about sixty-five million years ago, an asteroid measuring at least 6 miles (10 kilometers) wide struck Earth. The impact created a giant crater, started fires, and threw tons of dust and debris into the air. All the dust and smoke in the atmosphere kept sunlight from reaching Earth's surface. Many kinds of plants stopped growing, plant-eating animals could not find food and died, and animals that normally fed on the plant eaters had no food. Then most large animals, including dinosaurs, died out.

In recent centuries, humans have been the cause of much animal extinction. For instance, North America was once home to as many as three billion passenger pigeons. But starting in the nineteenth century, North American settlers cut down the vast forests where these birds made their homes. Without these forests, the birds could not find the nuts, berries, and other foods that they needed to survive. In addition, human hunters shot millions of passenger pigeons for food. This assault made it impossible for the surviving birds to find mates and produce offspring. By the early twentieth century, passenger pigeons were extinct.

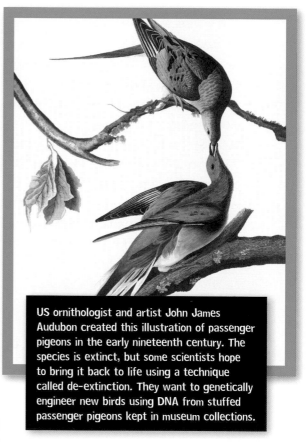

US ornithologist and artist John James Audubon created this illustration of passenger pigeons in the early nineteenth century. The species is extinct, but some scientists hope to bring it back to life using a technique called de-extinction. They want to genetically engineer new birds using DNA from stuffed passenger pigeons kept in museum collections.

Many animals of the twenty-first century are endangered, or on the brink of extinction. Giant pandas are an example. Pandas are native to the bamboo forests of China. But as loggers have cleared these forests for lumber and to make room for farmland, the numbers of giant pandas have plummeted. When species numbers drop, animals find it more difficult to locate mates. Many do not reproduce, so the species' overall population falls even more.

Experts are working to save some species from extinction by breeding the animals in nature preserves and zoos. Breeding involves putting males and females together in pens or other enclosures and encouraging them to mate. Some programs are working to see if modern medical technology such as in vitro fertilization (in which females are artificially impregnated without the animal engaging in sexual mating) could help save endangered species. Governments also try to prevent extinction by passing laws and protecting animal habitats, or natural environments. For instance, some laws prohibit the hunting of certain species. Sometimes governments establish wildlife preserves—areas that are off-limit to hunting, logging, farming, building, and other activities that would destroy habitat.

A WILD, WILD WORLD

Mutations, evolution, and natural selection have created the great variety of sexual practices and sexual equipment of the animal world. These sexual parts and practices emerged over many generations because they best enable animals to successfully produce offspring. Some of this equipment is straightforward, such as big penises that help males attract and impregnate females. But some of this equipment enables not more mating but more selective mating. For instance, male ducks frequently force sex on females. But female ducks, like many human females, don't want to bear the offspring of aggressive males that sexually assault

them. So the duck vagina has evolved to reject the sperm of such males. It is lined with spirals and pockets that trap sperm, preventing it from fertilizing eggs. But if a female duck does want a particular male to father her offspring, scientists think that she can relax muscles in her vagina to allow for fertilization.

Biologist and animal mating expert Carin Bondar remarks, "The diversity that we see in sexual structures in the animal kingdom that has evolved in response to the multitude of factors surrounding reproduction is pretty mind-blowing." In fact, some of the parts and practices involved in animal reproduction may seem strange, incredible, or downright gross, but to the animals themselves, they are essential for life. Animals with the best strategies for choosing mates, mingling eggs and sperm, and making babies help ensure that their species will continue into the future. Without animal sex, there would be no animal life.

The male peacock spider shakes his rainbow-colored tail in a bid to mate with a female.

CHAPTER 1
FANCY DANCERS

When humans shimmy and shake on the dance floor, they often do so to impress potential mates. The same is true in the animal world. Many animals make rhythmic movements to attract sexual partners. They stamp their hooves, flap their wings, or wag their heads and rear ends.

Sometimes both sexes join in the dance. For example, a male and female seahorse will swim side by side for several days, spinning and cartwheeling in unison before mating. When the dance is over, it's time to have sex. Male and female flamingos form a sort of dance troupe when they're ready to mate. Dozens of them march around the shallows in the lakes and marshes where they live, flipping their long pink necks and shiny black beaks from side to side. Mating follows shortly afterward.

LATIN FOR PIGS (AND EVERY OTHER SPECIES)

All plants and animals have common names, such as Shasta daisy or peacock spider. Biologists also use a scientific naming system created by Swedish scientist Carolus Linnaeus in the mid-eighteenth century. The system uses Latin-based terms to identify each plant or animal's genus (group) and species (specific kind within that group). For example, the scientific name for domestic dogs (of all breeds) is *Canis familiaris*. *Canis* is the genus name, and familiaris is the species name. The *Canis* genus also includes wolves (*Canis lupus*) and coyotes (*Canis latrans*).

Genus and species are the most precise classifications for living things. But these categories fall under a larger naming umbrella consisting of eight levels: domain, kingdom, phylum, class, order, family, genus, and species. You can see the hierarchy by looking at gray wolves. They belong to the domain Eukarya—a group that includes all plants and animals. Within that category, gray wolves belong to the kingdom Animalia (the animal kingdom), the phylum Chordata (animals with backbones), the class Mammalia (mammals, animals that give live birth and nurse their young), the order Carnivora (flesh-eating mammals), the family Canidae (doglike mammals), and the genus *Canis* (specific kinds of doglike mammals). The species name *Canis lupus* is the specific designation for the gray wolf. Each kind of living thing has its own species name, and members of the same species can mate with one another.

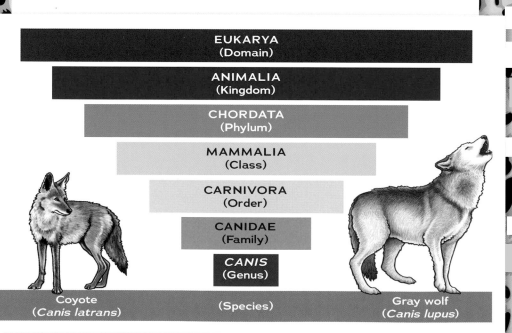

EUKARYA
(Domain)

ANIMALIA
(Kingdom)

CHORDATA
(Phylum)

MAMMALIA
(Class)

CARNIVORA
(Order)

CANIDAE
(Family)

CANIS
(Genus)

(Species)

Coyote
(*Canis latrans*)

Gray wolf
(*Canis lupus*)

But mostly, animal dancing is a male activity. Males dance to impress females, trying to woo them with their fancy moves.

SATURDAY NIGHT FEVER

Among satin bowerbirds (scientific name *Ptilonorhynchus violaceus*), which make their homes in the rain forests of eastern Australia, males not only dance to attract females, but they even build special "dance floors" for the performance. Weeks before mating season, the male satin bowerbird clears a space on the damp forest floor. Then he builds a bower, a two-walled structure formed from sticks and leaves

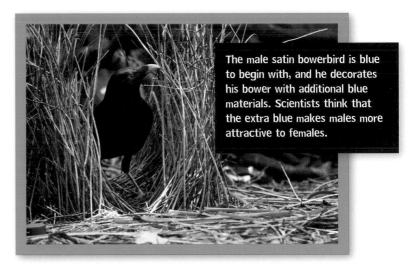

The male satin bowerbird is blue to begin with, and he decorates his bower with additional blue materials. Scientists think that the extra blue makes males more attractive to females.

and cemented together with his saliva. At the back of the bower, he creates a platform, also made of sticks and leaves, where he will perform his dance. He decorates the platform with blue objects: blue parrot feathers, blue-tinged snail shells, and blue flowers. Bowerbirds that live near populated areas might even use human-made blue objects, such as blue clothespins, bottle caps, ballpoint pens, coffee stirrers, drinking straws, and even Lego bricks.

Why blue? Biologists Stéphanie M. Doucet and Robert Montgomerie of Queen's University in Ontario, Canada, studied satin bowerbirds to find out. The birds have blue feathers, and the scientists learned that the more blue or ultraviolet (a color that is invisible to human eyes) a male has in his feathers, the healthier he will be. So the blue decorations in the bower might make the male seem even bluer and healthier—and therefore more attractive to females.

For weeks the male maintains his bower so it will be free of weeds and ready for mating season, which starts in November (springtime in Australia). When a female arrives to check out the bower, the male begins to dance. It's a bit like a robot dance, with rapid wingbeats accompanied by a mechanical croaking sound. He lowers his tail to the ground and bobs his head. Females that are sufficiently impressed will mate with the male.

FAN DANCERS

Many male birds, including peacocks, pheasants, and birds-of-paradise, fan out their tail feathers in a courtship dance to attract females. Scientists think that this display has roots in ancient animal history. Scientists studying fossilized dinosaur tailbones have determined that millions of years ago, some feathered dinosaurs (a group called the theropods) fanned out their tail feathers, possibly to attract mates. And since scientists know that birds are descended from dinosaurs, birds may have inherited tail fanning from their dinosaur ancestors.

PRESTO CHANGO

The male superb bird-of-paradise (*Lophorina superba*), a species that makes its home on the South Pacific island of New Guinea, goes through an amazing transformation to lure a mate. When he's interested in a female, he lifts his iridescent blue-green breast shield—a set of feathers along his chest. They fan out into an oblong shape that resembles a blue-green crescent moon. The male also flings his black back feathers upward to create an oval-shaped black cape. Finally, he tips his head back, lifting his black beak to create what appear to be two round blue eyes.

The Mating Dance Transformation of the Male Superb Bird-of-Paradise

Frontal View	Side View

1. The male superb bird-of-paradise normally looks like an ordinary bird.

2. His transformation begins when he lifts his iridescent blue-green breast shield and raises his blue-green crown freathers. The feathers of the breast shield fan out into a crescent-like shape.

3. He raises his black back feathers upward.

4. The back feathers fan out like a giant cape.

5. He tips his head back, lifting his black beak. It appears to divide his blue crown feathers, creating what look like two round blue eyes.

6. Then he is ready to impress a female with his mating dance.

When the male superb bird-of-paradise courts a female, fanning out his chest feathers and raising his back feathers, he takes on a bizarre appearance. This photo shows a female superb bird-of-paradise eyeing a male's impressive display.

The result is a look that a scientist at the Cornell University Laboratory of Ornithology (bird science) in New York calls a "psychedelic smiley face" on legs. The male then hops up and down around the female. He snaps his feathers the way people snap their fingers to make a popping sound.

The female's response? Most females are mainly indifferent, unimpressed, or downright cold to the display. The male superb bird-of-paradise is usually rejected by fifteen to twenty females before finding one that will mate with him.

ROCK AND ROLL

Devil rays (nine species in the genus *Mobula*) are winged fish related to sharks. They make their homes in oceans worldwide. When looking for sexual partners, devil rays—which can weigh as much as 1 ton (0.9 metric tons)—leap up from beneath the water and spin around in the air. They have velvety black backs and bright white undersides, so when they flip, they look like spinning strobe lights. After flipping, they land back on the water with a slap—the louder the better.

The point is to prove they're big and strong—a signal to potential mates that they're the healthiest and the best. Like other animals, they're strutting their stuff—and among devil rays, that stuff is giant wings, heavy bodies, and the ability to throw themselves into the air. These are the qualities a ray wants to share with a mate to produce the finest offspring.

According to a TV show called *Shark*, produced by the British Broadcasting Corporation (BBC), rays like to make a big splash. The show's narrator explains, "As

Devil rays will leap from the water, spin in the air, and land with a loud slap. The ray that puts on the most dramatic display is most likely to attract mates.

they land, the impact sends a huge boom through the water. The higher they leap, the bigger the bang. It's mainly males that jump like this, signaling their prowess as a mate. Females also join in [the jumping], drawing attention to themselves. It's thought that those that make the biggest impact on the spectators [the opposite sex] give themselves the best odds of leaving with a mate."

GOOD VIBRATIONS

The tiny peacock spider (*Maratus volans*), which is the size of a pea, is a native of Australia. Like all spiders, it has eight legs. Six of the legs (the four front-most legs and the two in back) are gray, while the second legs from the back are black with white tips. The black legs do the talking when the male peacock spider is ready to start his mating dance. He raises them high in a bid for attention. With a female's eyes on him, he then raises his bright, rainbow-hued tail. He shimmies it in a fast vibration to win the affection of the female.

He also thumps his feet on the ground, sending her more good vibrations. He sometimes walks toward her and even drums his feet on her head. The dance can last between four and fifty minutes. A successful male peacock spider might win several females with this display. But if the female does not find the advances attractive, she might eat the male.

RHYTHM SECTION

Female Atlantic cod (*Gadus morhua*), residents of Atlantic and Arctic waters, lay different clutches, or groups, of eggs over a period of several months. A female can lay up to one million eggs a season. Males fertilize the eggs as soon as they're laid. But a female won't let just any male near her eggs. She doesn't release them until she has chosen a proper mate.

To win the female's approval, groups of male cod swim in circles around her. To attract her attention, they use muscles on the outside of their swim bladders (organs that help them

control how deep they go in the ocean) to make a rhythmic drumming noise. The female allows only certain males to get close enough to swim below her. A male that is allowed to get close will grasp her with his fins until she releases her eggs, which he will then fertilize with

ARACHNOPHILIA

Jürgen Otto, an entomologist (a scientist who studies insects) and photographer from the Australian Institute of Marine Science near Townsville, Australia, was the first to film the mating dance of the peacock spider. Many people have told him that seeing such a cute, furry spider in action (one scientist calls them "kittens with too many legs") has helped their arachnophobia (fear of spiders), allowing them to warm up to spiders.

his sperm. Other males hover around, jockeying for position, but aren't allowed near enough to fertilize the eggs.

How does the female choose? To find out, biologists Sherrylynn Rowe and Jeffrey A. Hutchings of Dalhousie University in Nova Scotia, Canada, studied cod from the Scotian Shelf, an area of the Atlantic Ocean. They brought cod into laboratory aquariums and observed them both visually and auditorily, using a hydrophone to pick up the sound of the animal's underwater drumming. The scientists found that the sound of the drumming varied from male to male and from place to place.

In one group of cod, which the scientists named 4T, the males were territorial about their surroundings and possessive about their females. Males in 4X, another group, didn't show as much aggression but made more noise. The scientists observed that the 4X males had bigger, stronger drumming muscles than those in 4T. And those with the biggest drumming muscles had more success in mating.

The male Morelet's tree frog sings to attract females. The sound travels through both air and water.

CHAPTER 2
LOVE SONGS

The animal world is full of loudmouths. Animals that vocalize—through singing, yelling, croaking, and other sounds—include birds, whales, walruses, frogs, and insects. Animals use calls for many reasons: to establish territory, to announce their membership in a group, and to coordinate defenses against predators.

But that's not all. In the animal kingdom, males often use their voices to show reproductive fitness—to show females that in choosing them, the females are getting a really good deal. The male with the loudest voice or the longest call may be the strongest or largest, and females often choose their mates accordingly. Scientists have found that when it comes to animal

PECKING ORDER

In 1995 the National Aeronautics and Space Administration (NASA) delayed the launch of space shuttle *Discovery* for several weeks, at a cost of nearly $1 million. Why? A flock of male yellow-shafted flickers, a species of woodpecker, had mistaken the shuttle for a tree. The flickers punched about seventy holes in the space shuttle's orange foam skin while it was sitting on the launchpad at Cape Canaveral, Florida.

Using their bills, woodpeckers peck holes in trees to find food and to build nests. Males also peck as a mating ritual. The sound and frequency of their pecking demonstrates their strength and size to females within earshot. The incident at Cape Canaveral occurred during spring nesting season, and scientists believe the birds were trying to attract females with their pecking noise.

To scare off the shuttle-pecking flickers, NASA had installed owl decoys and owl hoot recordings. (Owls prey on woodpeckers.) But the flickers ignored them all. "The little birds [the woodpeckers] got the better of the big birds [the aerospace program]," NASA spokesman Bruce Buckingham joked.

mating calls, any extreme—the loudest, longest, deepest, or most varied song—is most likely to attract the opposite sex. Males also use their voices to warn other males to back off—telling them to stay away from available females.

FROGGIE WENT A-COURTIN'

In the fine art of the serenade—a love song thrown out to lure a mate to come close—the male tree frog is king. He uses his melodious chirping to signal his gender, his readiness to mate, his fitness to do so, the size of his geographic territory, and his real-time location. Frogs are amphibians, which means that they live both on land and in water, so the male tree frog is able to send his song through air and water. Every species of tree frog has its own distinct song, with regional differences depending on location.

CRITTERCAM

Scientists have never observed humpback males mating in the wild. To learn more about humpback mating, oceanographer Louis Herman of the Dolphin Institute in Honolulu, Hawaii, used a device called a Crittercam. This is a stick-on video camera equipped with suction cups. From their boat, Herman and his team used a long pole to attach a Crittercam to the back of a male humpback off the coast of the Hawaiian island of Maui.

As the whale swam off, the camera filmed a group of males chasing and bashing one another out of the way to get close to a lone female. The males slapped the water with their tails, threw their heads back and forth, blew out clouds of bubbles from their blowholes, and shouldered one another from side to side. Eventually, the female sidled up to the male that seemed to have impressed her most by his forceful display—which in this case was the male with the Crittercam.

At some point after the couple got together, the lead male knocked the camera off his body, so the scientists couldn't observe actual mating. The Crittercam was equipped with a flotation device and a radio transmitter. It rose to the ocean's surface, and the scientists in the boat retrieved it.

Male humpback whales sing to attract females and also to warn off male rivals.

Female tree frogs know how to interpret the songs of their species, and they respond to the calls that appeal to them.

Biologist Venetia S. Briggs of the University of Miami in Florida has studied the calls of male Morelet's tree frogs (*Agalychnis moreletii*). These small frogs live in forests and wetlands in Mexico and Central America and are recognizable by their white-spotted green trunks and their peach-colored bellies. Briggs observed that like other tree frogs, male Morelet's frogs use different calls for different reasons. Some songs attract mates. Other songs warn rival males to keep their distance. Briggs notes that males look for mates just after sunset. They descend from the trees where they live, gather at ponds, and call to females with a sound that Briggs describes as a "zworp."

LOUD AND CLEAR

The world's largest mammals—whales—have elaborate mating songs. Humpback whales (*Megaptera novaeangliae*), which are native to the Pacific, Atlantic, Indian, and Southern Oceans, can grow to be 62 feet (19 meters) long. While researchers cannot say for sure what every whale song means, they know that some songs are used in mating and others are used as warnings to sexual rivals.

In one study, researchers J. D. Darling of Whale Trust Maui and Martine Bérubé of the University of Groningen in the Netherlands played recordings of male humpback whale songs to other males. They found that some whales changed course to avoid the sounds while others charged aggressively toward the sounds. The research suggested that male humpbacks use their songs to establish dominance and hierarchy within the pod (a social grouping of whales).

Male humpbacks might also sing to attract females for sex. A male can sing for more than two hours, perhaps to show a female that such an expenditure of energy is nothing for him. A long song is a sign of the male's strength, lung power, size, and stamina—all of which might appeal to a female whale.

Most male humpback whales sing the same song during each breeding season, which lasts from winter to early spring. At some point, however, a male might innovate, singing a different pattern or tune. Why would a male whale change his tune during breeding season? Some researchers theorize that a new song might make a male seem like an outsider—an animal that is not related to the main group. An outsider would appeal to a female because breeding within a small group, generation after generation, can lead to health problems in a population. Every whale in the pod might carry genes for a disease or other ailment. A female could avoid passing such genes to her offspring by mating outside the usual population. Female humpbacks (and other animals) most likely use instinct rather than conscious behavior when they choose outsiders as mates. This behavior gives them the best chance of giving birth to healthy offspring.

SQUEAK UP

While humans can hear whale songs loud and clear, the songs of mice (family Muridae) are ultrasonic. That means they are mostly out of human hearing range, although other mice can hear the songs. In North Carolina, Duke University researcher Erich Jarvis and his team used ultrasound microphones and software to analyze mouse songs. They found that male mice sing to attract mates and that the songs change depending on the situation. For instance, if a male mouse is wooing a female that is in view, he will sing a simple mating song of just a few notes. If the female is not in view but the male can smell that she's in estrus, or heat (ready for sex), he'll raise his voice and add details such as extra notes and syllables to make his song more complex.

By recording songs and playing them back to females, the researchers found that female mice were drawn to more complex songs. The researchers also observed that once a male had gotten a female to come close, the singing stopped and sexual activity began.

IN THE HEAT OF THE MOMENT

Estrus occurs in most species of mammals (although not in humans and some kinds of apes). During estrus, the hormone estrogen stimulates the female body to produce eggs. The hormone also sends an olfactory (smell) message to males of the species. The smell tells males that the female is fertile and ready to receive his sperm.

The frequency of estrus depends on the species. Small mammals, such as mice, go into heat every four to five days year-round, stopping only when they are pregnant. Some larger animals, such as bears, are in heat only once a year, during the spring. A few mammals, such as rabbits, are fertile all the time. They are always in estrus unless they are pregnant.

The human menstrual cycle, which occurs about once every twenty-eight days in women of childbearing age, is similar to estrus. In humans and other mammals, when a female produces an egg, the uterus grows a layer of tissue called the endometrium, which will protect and nourish a fertilized egg as it develops into a fetus. In animals with a menstrual cycle, the endometrium flows out of the female's body (through monthly menstruation) if the egg is not fertilized. In animals with an estrus cycle, the endometrium is reabsorbed into the body if the egg is not fertilized. Animals with estrus cycles have sex only when they are in heat. Animals with menstrual cycles may be sexually active at any time.

A male hammerhead bat will honk loudly through its lips and snout, hoping to attract females for sex.

NOSE JOB

Trying to get someone's attention? You might try honking your car horn. That's what male hammerhead bats (*Hypsignathus monstrosus*) do when they're looking to mate—although they honk with their snouts, lips, and extra-large larynxes (voice boxes) instead of car horns. Hammerheads live in regions around the equator in Africa. For four months out of every year, the males of the species gather by the dozen, jockeying for position among trees above streams, where they hang out and honk at the girls.

These bats are enormous, with wingspans stretching more than 3 feet (1 m). The faces of the males have big hammer-like snouts, for which the bats are named. (Females have daintier faces, and they don't honk.) The biggest schnozzes make the loudest honks and attract the most females. When a female comes near, a male will then change his call, making what Cornell University ecologist Jack Bradbury describes as a "staccato buzz—a very, very loud rapid buzzing sound."

If a female likes what she hears, she'll approach the male for a thirty- to sixty-second mating session. While holding her from behind, the male will insert his penis into her vagina. (Some species of bats perform oral sex before mating, stimulating each other's genitals with their mouths. Scientists have noted that this practice leads to prolonged copulation, or sexual intercourse.) If the female is impregnated, she will deliver one baby about 120 days later. Females usually give birth twice a year.

Some males are more successful with females than others. Studies have shown that in hammerhead colonies, just a small group of males (6 percent) will father most of the bat pups (79 percent).

Two male marine iguanas battle for mating rights. The fight involves wrestling and biting.

CHAPTER 3
WRESTLEMANIA!

Fighting for love? It's not uncommon in the animal kingdom. Male giraffes, for instance, stage neck battles to see which one will win the female. During these battles, they cross necks as if they were swords. The bouts can result in broken necks, broken jaws, and on rare occasions even death. Male marine iguanas ward off rivals by bobbing their heads fiercely, a move that other males view as a threat. If that doesn't work, the males will battle by butting their heads together, shoving, and wrestling.

In certain species, a male's horns, antlers, claws, or tusks are much bigger than those of the females of the same species. Males often use this equipment to fight one another for mates. For her part, a female might size up a male's physical traits, such as his antlers or tusks, and choose a mate with the biggest weapons.

CRACKING SKULLS

Among bighorn sheep (*Ovis canadensis*), which are native to western Canada, the western United States, and Mexico, the rams will knock heads together to determine which one gets to mate with a particular ewe (female). Every time a male bighorn sheep cracks skulls with another male, the impact generates about 760 pounds (345 kilograms) of force—comparable to the force of a punch by a professional boxer. Unlike humans, bighorn rams aren't susceptible to concussions and don't seem to experience pain from these collisions.

Bighorn rams butt heads in battles that can last for several hours. The victorious ram wins the right to mate with females.

Scientists say that the secret is in the rams' horns. The horns are made of an outer layer of keratin (the same substance of human fingernails and toenails) over an inner layer of porous bone. (Porous materials allow liquids and air to pass through them.) Engineers Parimal Maity and Srinivasan Tekalur of Michigan State University used computer imaging to build a three-dimensional model of a bighorn ram's horn. Then they analyzed how the horn responded to 760 pounds (345 kg) of force. Maity and Tekalur found that the bighorn's horn is very good at absorbing shock because it is elastic, or flexible. The porous bony core and the keratin sheath work together to absorb energy and to protect the ram's brain during collisions.

EYES ON THE PRIZE

While bighorn males use their horns, stalk-eyed flies use their legs to fight for females. Members of the family Diopsidae, the flies make their homes near streams throughout Southeast Asia and southern Africa. As the name implies, these flies have eyes on stalks. The eyestalks extend from the sides of the fly's head. Male eyestalks are longer than those of the females. In some cases, the male's eye span (the distance between his eyes) is greater than the length of his body.

Male stalk-eyed flies fight one another for food and for mates. During fights they face each other, keeping their eyestalks parallel to each other and bobbing their abdomens up and down. They rise on their hind legs and use their forelegs to jab the other fly's face. They might try to hook a leg

Two male stalk-eyed flies face off in a battle for mating rights in South Africa.

and upend the other fly. In observing these fights, biologists Tami Panhuis and Gerald Wilkinson of the University of Maryland noted that males with larger eye spans won more bouts, no matter

QUICK-CHANGE ARTISTS

Some animals use amazing tricks to attract mates and repel enemies. Examples include squid, which come in a variety of colors, depending on the species. Using pigments in their skin cells, squid can change their colors for camouflage—to blend into their surroundings for protection from predators. Male squid also change colors to attract females and to fend off competing males.

For example, the market squid is usually whitish, but the male's arms and head will turn bright red during sex. Other male squid perceive the red as a warning to stay away. The Caribbean reef squid is greenish brown. The male of the species turns white to fend off other males and changes to red to attract females. He sometimes even splits into two colors—red on the side of his body facing his potential mate and white on the side facing approaching males.

Cuttlefish, a marine animal related to squid, can also change colors for camouflage or to send messages to other cuttlefish. When mating, a male cuttlefish might show distinctive male skin patterns to females on one side of his body while displaying typical female patterns to males on the other side. With this disguise, he attracts females from one side. Meanwhile, competitive males, viewing him from the other side, think that he's a female, not a rival male. They don't rush in to disrupt his mating efforts.

which fly had a bigger body. The males with the larger eye spans also won their fights faster.

In another experiment, biologists Dietrich Burkhardt and Ingrid de la Motte of the University of Regensburg in Germany tested whether females preferred males with big eye spans. The scientists killed males by freezing them, then mounted them on threads, in natural positions, two inside each cage. These were the dummy males: one with an eye span of about 0.3 inches (8.5 millimeters) and one with an eye span of about 0.4 inches (10.5 mm). Each night at dusk (mating time for the flies), the scientists introduced two females into each cage. Of the ninety-six females tested, sixty-five landed on the thread of the dummy with the bigger eye span. As the University of Maryland study showed, males with the larger eye spans are the winningest fighters, so that might be why females prefer them.

DAD OF THE YEAR

Male three-spined sticklebacks (*Gasterosteus aculeatus*) will fight for mating rights and also fight to protect their offspring. These fish have three sharp fins along their spines and live in northern waters worldwide. They live in the mouths of rivers and along ocean coasts. In March and April, the male three-spined stickleback, which most of the year is brownish and drab, undergoes a profound transformation. His eyes change from light blue to shiny aquamarine. He develops a glittery red throat and belly. These spiffy new duds are designed to attract females.

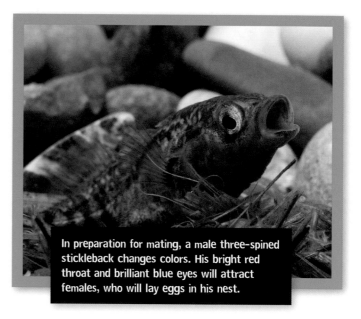

In preparation for mating, a male three-spined stickleback changes colors. His bright red throat and brilliant blue eyes will attract females, who will lay eggs in his nest.

Once the male has adopted his new colors, he's ready to leave the shoals (sandbars) of his territory and build a nest where one or more females can lay eggs. He builds this nest with stringy algae and sand, which he plasters together with spiggin, a type of glue that his kidneys secrete.

In the course of building their nests, male sticklebacks might raid other males' nests to steal nesting material. And once females have laid their eggs, males will try to sneak into other males' nests immediately, to fertilize the eggs before the nest owners can do so. If another male has already fertilized the eggs, a competing male might steal them and eat them. Or he might move them to his own nest, which will attract additional females to lay their eggs there. All these activities help males increase their number of offspring while decreasing the number of offspring produced by their rivals.

Scientists have found that large male sticklebacks have fewer rivals than small ones. In one study, biologists Ulrika Candolin and Heinz-Rudolf Voigt of the University of Helsinki in Finland found that big stickleback males control the largest territories in the stickleback world. They had fewer male rivals, and more females laid eggs in their nests. These were the males the females preferred, probably because by choosing these dominant fish as fathers, the females gave their offspring a better chance at survival.

Once eggs are in the nest, male sticklebacks tend to the eggs by keeping the nests clean and by fanning water over them to increase the amount of life-giving oxygen reaching the eggs. The fathers chase away rival males to defend the eggs, guarding them until they hatch.

SWITCH HITTERS

Flatworms live in waters all over the world. A few species live on land. Some flatworms can reproduce asexually, with one individual breaking in two and with each piece regenerating a new head or tail. But most flatworms reproduce sexually. They are hermaphrodites, so they have the reproductive organs of both males and females.

Some species of flatworms, such as the colorful marine-dwelling *Pseudoceros bifurcus*, mate via a tough battle called penis

TWO-WAY STREETS

Hermaphroditic animals include snails, flatworms, slugs, and barnacles. From a survival standpoint, hermaphroditism makes sense. If an animal can mate with any other member of its species, using either its male or female sex organs, it increases its chances of successful reproduction. It's much easier to find a mate if you're not limited to the opposite sex. Some hermaphroditic animals, such as tapeworms, can even use their male and female sexual equipment to impregnate themselves.

fencing. Sitting on their tails, two flatworms will raise their upper bodies and face each other. They brandish their double-headed, white-tipped penises and then strike out at each other. The fencing bout can last up to an hour, with each worm stabbing the other multiple times with its spike-tipped penis.

The battle ends when one or both worms succeed not only in piercing the other's body but also in injecting sperm into the gash. In this way, one or both worms become impregnated. A pregnant flatworm will begin eating right away, feeding on small creatures called sea squirts, to store up nutrients for its developing offspring. It will lay a mass of several hundred eggs, which hatch about ten days later.

A male Antarctic penguin presents a pebble to a female. She will use the gift, along with many other pebbles, to build a nest.

CHAPTER 4
VALENTINE'S DAY

In the human world, if you don't have the dance moves, size, good looks, or physical prowess to get the nod from the person you want to date, you may resort to giving gifts. Some animals use this technique as well. Biologists have a name for such presents: nuptial gifts. It's the males that offer nuptial gifts to the females, hoping to entice them to mate.

Usually a nuptial gift consists of food, but sometimes—as with katydids—the package of food also contains sperm. This gift nourishes the female and also impregnates her. Antarctic penguins build nests from pebbles, and to win a female's affection, a male Antarctic penguin might give her a pebble as a gift. Regardless of the present—whether it consists of food or something else—all gift-giving animals have the same goal: sex.

TRICK OR TREAT?

Nursery-web spiders (*Pisaura mirabilis*), natives of Europe, get their name because the mothers take very good care of their eggs, sheltering them in a protective web. When he's hoping to mate, a male nursery-web spider has to woo a female very carefully. If she's bigger than he is and if she has mated before, she might be aggressive toward him. To get on her good side, the male will approach her with a present—a small dead insect or another spider wrapped in fine silk. (Spiders produce their own silk using fingerlike structures called spinnerets.) The gift might be as big as he is.

MYSTERY CIRCLES

For years scientists and divers couldn't figure out what was making intricate circular patterns in the sand on the ocean floor near Amami Oshima, an island off the coast of Japan. Divers first spotted the patterns in 1995 and called them mystery circles. In 2011 and 2012, a team from a natural history museum in Chiba, Japan, used underwater still and video cameras to monitor the circles. The scientists carried the cameras with them while scuba diving to the seafloor several times a day. They also left behind video cameras to monitor the circles in their absence.

The secret artist, finally captured on video, was a tiny, nondescript puffer fish, a poisonous fish native to coastal Japan. The fish swam back and forth, sweeping his fins and tail through the sand to make a wheel-shaped circle. The 7-foot-wide (2.1 m) circle was more than twenty times longer than the fish itself. The fish then used his lips to pick up shells and pieces of sand of different sizes and colors, which he deposited to decorate the wheel. The swimming artist worked on his project for a week or more.

If the female accepts his nuptial gift, the male can begin mating. He will insert his pedipalps (appendages designed for both eating and reproduction) into the female's epigynum (genitals), on the underside of her abdomen, and transfer his sperm to her.

But if the female is aggressive, the male might try to trick her into mating. He will play dead, a practice called thanatosis. (*Thanatos* means "death" in Greek.) He holds onto his nuptial gift with his mouthparts, remaining motionless, with his legs fully extended. The female, thinking the male is dead, will take the gift and start to leave. At this point, the faker will jump back up and try to mate again. Playing dead gives males a second chance at sex.

In experiments conducted in 2007, biologist Trine Bilde and

Scientists have since learned that when female puffer fish are ready to release their eggs, they look for such a wheel. The male that created it ushers the female toward its center. He fluffs the sand there to make it soft for her eggs. When she is at the center, the male bites her cheek to hold her in place. Then she releases her eggs, while he releases his sperm into the water around them. The sperm swim to the eggs and fertilize them. The female swims off when the spawning (the depositing and fertilizing of fish eggs) is finished. The male stays to care for the fertilized eggs until they hatch.

A male puffer fish *(seen at center)* created this elaborate design on the seafloor off the coast of Japan. Males make these sandy circles to entice females to deposit eggs there. The males then fertilize the eggs.

her colleagues at Aarhus University in Denmark found thanatosis to be highly effective. She noted that 100 percent of the males that played dead as part of the nuptial ritual succeeded in mating with the female. Males that did not perform thanatosis were far less successful in having sex with the female spider.

Playing dead is not the only trick male nursery-web spiders rely on when mating. The nuptial gift itself may be a dud, containing inedible plant seeds, flowers, or the husk of a dead insect rather than a juicy live fly. Offering a gift—whether a good one or a disappointment—gives a male more time with a female. While she's unwrapping her gift, he begins the sex act. Maria J. Albo, another biologist at Aarhus University, compared mating success among male nursery-web spiders. Albo found that males offering worthless gifts, such as an inedible plant part, were just as successful at mating as those offering a live fly. But males offering no gift at all had very few matings.

For her part, when the female nursery-web spider discovers that her nuptial gift is a dud, she terminates the sex act, shoving the male away. But by then, the male may already have introduced his sperm into her body.

HUNGRY FOR LOVE

Katydids (family Tettigoniidae), a type of grasshopper, are native to every continent except Antarctica. In the katydid mating ritual, the male gives the female a two-part nuptial gift. In preparation for mating, the body of the male katydid produces a structure called a spermatophore. It contains an ampulla (a small globule of sperm) and a spermatophylax (a larger sac of gelatinous nutrients). When the female accepts and gathers the spermatophylax to her mouthparts, the male puts the ampulla into her genitals.

The food in a single spermatophylax can fuel the female for

about two days. During this time, she doesn't need to feed on leaves or insects as she normally would. She can stay at home on a tree or bush, hidden from predators, without venturing out in the open to look for food.

The spermatophore can equal one-third of the male katydid's body mass, and the bigger the male, the bigger his spermatophore. Females prefer heavier males, because they have the largest spermatophores, which means more nutrition for the mother and for her developing eggs.

BUTCHER BIRDS

Great gray shrikes also offer food gifts. These birds are sometimes called northern shrikes (*Lanius excubitor*), and they are native to Europe and North America. They feed on rodents, smaller birds, lizards, and insects. They don't always eat this food right away, however. Instead, the birds impale their prey on thorns, branches, or barbed wire, creating a kind of "butcher shop." This food can be eaten (or fed to nestlings) later, when prey might be scarce. When a male great gray shrike is wooing a female, he impresses her with the size of his butcher shop, which shows her that he is strong and healthy. He turns to face her and flutters his wings.

A male great gray shrike has killed a mouse and impaled it on a branch. He might eat the mouse himself or present it to a female as a nuptial gift.

PANDA PORN

Pandas are large black-and-white mammals that live in mountainous areas of central China. Because of farming, logging, and other human development, the panda is endangered. About sixteen hundred pandas still live in the wild, and about three hundred pandas live in zoos and wildlife centers, mostly in China.

Wanting to save giant pandas from extinction, scientists try to mate them in captivity. Female pandas go into estrus only once a year, for several days in the spring. During these times, at Chengdu Research Base of Giant Panda Breeding in China's Sichuan Province, zookeepers put male and female pandas together in the same space, hoping the animals will mate naturally. But keepers have noted that often the animals show little interest in sex. What's more, the inactivity of living in captivity has weakened the pandas' legs to the point where even males that want to mate don't have the leg strength to stay in position long enough to have intercourse.

Keepers have tackled these problems by exercising the male pandas, having them climb up and down heavy log ladders to build up leg strength. Keepers have also

Giant pandas are an endangered species. To increase the panda population, zookeepers and researchers put male and female pandas together, hoping they will mate and produce offspring.

shown the males videos of other pandas mating. This "panda porn" increases the males' sex drive, and their new leg strength helps them stay in position during copulation. As a result, more female pandas have become pregnant through sex.

To increase numbers even more, scientists at the research center have also impregnated pandas using artificial insemination. This procedure bypasses sex altogether. Instead, scientists surgically take sperm from a male and transfer it to the womb of a female panda when she is in estrus. If the procedure results in a successful pregnancy, a baby panda will be born about fifty days later.

He then calls to her and offers a food gift from his butcher shop. After she accepts his gift, the two have sex.

A male and a female great gray shrike that have mated will build a nest and raise young together, but the male isn't always faithful to his nestmate. He may offer gifts from his butcher shop to another female and mate with her on the side. In a study conducted in the early twenty-first century, researchers from Poland and the Czech Republic found that males offered more nutritious gifts to these "other women" than they offered to their own nestmates. The researchers think that the males benefited by this arrangement by having more offspring without having to defend another nest or care for more hatchlings. For the females that cheat with the males, the benefit is the extra-nutritious food.

WHAT'S FOR DINNER?

If you see a male kingfisher (*Alcedo atthis*) with the head of a fish protruding from his beak (meaning the tail is in his mouth), it's a sure sign that he's about to feed the fish to a female kingfisher. Scientists call this practice courtship feeding.

Kingfishers live near rivers and lakes and in forests in many parts of the world, especially in tropical areas. They mostly eat fish, which they usually swallow headfirst (except when a male is courtship feeding a female). Some kinds of kingfishers also eat frogs, salamanders, tadpoles, and insects.

Some researchers think that courtship feeding strengthens the bond between kingfisher mates. Other scientists say that courtship feeding allows female kingfishers to conserve their strength. By relying on their mates for food, females don't have to expend energy diving for fish. They can put this extra energy into producing and laying eggs.

Biologists William Davis and Douglas Graham of the Smithsonian Tropical Research Institute in Panama, in Central

America, followed twelve pairs of Amazon kingfishers to learn more about their mating habits. The researchers found that as the time to lay eggs drew near, female kingfishers became less and less active, allowing the males to feed them. Female birds whose mates fed them more laid more eggs, but females whose mates fed them less laid few if any eggs. This study seems to support the theory that courtship feeding is necessary for kingfishers to produce offspring.

Male arctiid moths release pheromones from four hairy coremata tubes extending from the back of their bodies. The scent attracts females, which release their own pheromones.

CHAPTER 5
CHEMISTRY SETS

Looking for love? Well, don't make a big stink about it—unless you're an animal that uses odor to bring mates to your yard. Then pheromones—airborne chemicals that signal that you're ready for mating—are all you need. Many animals, large and small, communicate with these chemicals.

Animals produce pheromones for two purposes: to broadcast a "come-hither, let's mate" message to the opposite sex of the same species and to send "back off" messages to romantic rivals. Pheromones are species-specific concoctions. They communicate messages that are readable only by organisms with neurons (nerve cells) specifically adapted to receive them. Animals may notice pheromones from other species, but they can't read the messages in the scent.

Different animals release pheromones in different ways. Some animals emit the chemicals in their urine or feces. Others emit them through glands or hairs designed specifically for that purpose. Animals also detect pheromones using different body parts. For instance, insects smell pheromones through receptors in their antennae. Many mammals detect pheromones using their sense of smell or taste.

THE NOSE KNOWS

Insects have between 10,000 and 100,000 olfactory (smell) receptor neurons on their antennae. That might sound like a lot, but compare that number to the 6 million such neurons in the human nose. And that total is dwarfed by the amount of olfactory receptor neurons in a dog's snout: more than 220 million.

ARCTIID AROMA

Many insects produce pheromones. An example is the arctiid moth (*Creatonotos gangis*), a native of Southeast Asia and Australia. The moth life cycle is complex. Like many other kinds of insects, moths go through several physical stages, known collectively as metamorphosis. In the first stage, after hatching from eggs, moths take the form of wormlike caterpillars. During molting, the caterpillars shed their skin several times as they grow. During the next stage, caterpillars grow a protective shell made of a tough, protective substance called the chitin. Some caterpillars (including arctiid moth caterpillars) also spin protective cocoons from their own silk. Inside its chitin and cocoon, the moth is called a pupa. After a period ranging from a few days to several months, depending on the species, the insect emerges from its coverings as a full-grown winged moth.

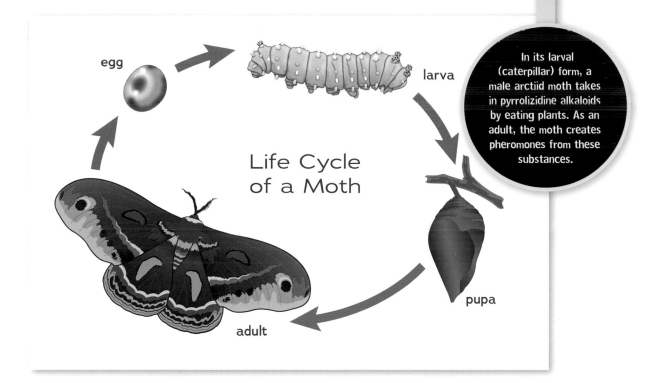

Life Cycle of a Moth

egg

larva

In its larval (caterpillar) form, a male arctiid moth takes in pyrrolizidine alkaloids by eating plants. As an adult, the moth creates pheromones from these substances.

pupa

adult

The male arctiid moth begins to create its pheromones early on in its metamorphosis. In caterpillar form, the male ingests pyrrolizidine alkaloids, substances produced by the leafy plants the caterpillar eats. The moth's body creates pheromones from these substances.

Arctiid moths mate at night, and researchers Michael Boppré and Dietrich Schneider of the Max Planck Institute for Behavioral Physiology in Germany used night-vision cameras to observe this mating. The scientists discovered that when a male arctiid moth catches the pheromone scent of a female, he releases pheromones from four appendages called coremata tubes. He first displays the tubes, which look like long-haired pipe cleaners that arc from his rear end. An air bladder at the base of the tubes helps force out the scent. In response, the female produces her own pheromones, communicating with males that she is ready to mate.

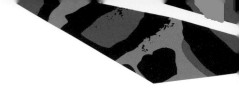

BLOWIN' IN THE WIND

Silkworm moths are native to China. In caterpillar form, these insects are called silkworms, because they spin cocoons made of silk threads. More than four thousand years ago, people in China learned how to turn these cocoons into silk cloth. In modern times, breeders raise one species of silkworm moth (*Bombyx mori*) in captivity and use the moths to breed silkworms for making silk.

When a male silkworm is ready to mate, he sends out a type of pheromone called an aphrodisiac. Scientists think that hair pencils—small structures under the male's front legs—secrete the chemical substance. The aphrodisiac triggers the female's body to produce its own sex pheromones. Neurons in male silkworm moths' antennae are specially adapted to detect the smell. When the male smells a female, he shifts his body so that he's facing the wind—in the direction of the female, with her smell wafting toward him. He follows this smell to the female.

When he finds her, he sets his wings madly fluttering. (Silkworm moths can't fly.) He sidles up to her and curves his abdomen toward hers. The two moths press their genital openings together, and his sperm enters her body. The impregnated female will lay between three hundred and five hundred eggs. She'll die shortly after laying them.

CRABS AND MUSCULAR MUSSELS

New Zealand pea crabs (*Pinnotheres novaezelandiae*) also use pheromones to invite mating. These small crabs live inside the shells of green-lipped mussels, which make their homes in the coastal waters around New Zealand.

Pea crabs are parasites. In a parasitic relationship, one creature lives inside or on the body of another, gaining benefits from its host. For example, male and female pea crabs live off food that the mussel traps in its gills. They also are safe from predators inside the mussel's shell.

Normally, only one pea crab lives inside one mussel—except at mating time. That's when the male crab leaves the shelter of his own personal mussel host to go in search of a mate. Mussels have two shells and a strong muscle that holds them shut. The shells can slam together like a steel trap, pulverizing crabs that are trying to get in or out.

Scientists wondered how crabs—facing the threat of pulverization—move safely in and out of mussel shells. Finally, in 2015, biologists Oliver Trottier and Andrew G. Jeffs from the University of Auckland in New Zealand captured pea crab mating behavior on night-vision video. The scientists placed mussels containing female crabs upstream from mussels with male crabs to see whether the males would know the females were there. Sure enough, they did. The females' pheromones, released when the females were ready to mate, inspired 60 percent of the males to emerge from their own mussel hosts and travel to the females. The biologists observed that the males squeezed out through gaps in the valves that keep the mussel shells locked.

The nighttime video footage also showed how male crabs got into the mussels that contain females. They tickled the mussels along the edges of their shells for up to four hours at a time! "The male crab [keeps] rubbing the same place until it goes numb," explained Trottier. Finally, after all this rubbing and tickling, the mussels opened their shells and let the male pea crabs in to mate with the females.

The timing of the tickling seems to be deliberate. It tends to happen during the dark of night, when mussels seem to be less sensitive. During the daytime, they are more likely to slam their shells shut and crush a male pea crab. The researchers think that night is also safer than daytime for crabs because, sitting outside a mussel shell, they are less visible to predators in the darkness.

Once inside the shell, the male and female crabs mate by embracing, abdomen to abdomen. Using appendages called pleopods, the male transfers sperm into the female's spermatheca. She'll keep the sperm in this holding sac until her eggs are ready for fertilization.

SHELL GAME

American lobsters (*Homarus americanus*), native to the western North Atlantic Ocean, emit pheromones through their urine. The urine contains different chemicals depending on whether the lobster is male or female and whether it is interested in loving or fighting. A female lobster passes the word that she is ready to mate by sending a stream of fragrant urine into her neighborhood.

Lobsters' bodies are protected by hard shells. As they grow, lobsters molt several times. Before they shed their shells, a new shell forms under the old one. At first, the new shell is soft (making the animal vulnerable to predators), but it hardens over several months. Before they are seven years old, lobsters molt more than twenty times. After that, molting slows down to about once a year.

Female lobsters mate only after molting, but males can mate before or after molting. Using naturalistic observation tanks, marine biologist Jelle Atema of the Marine Biological Laboratory in Woods Hole, Massachusetts, watched the mating up close. He noted that a female will scope out her surroundings and select the mate she wants (usually the largest male around) when she is ready to mate. Then she pees outside his rocky den. She uses her gills to blow the scented fluid toward him. Pheromones in the urine tell the male that she is ready for sex. The male receives the female's urine message through hairs on his antennae.

The male waves his swimmerets, small appendages under

his abdomen, to pull the scent in and consider the offer. If he likes what he senses, he comes out of his den with his front claws raised. The hen (female lobster) may fight back at first, but eventually she touches her claws to the top of his head to signal her readiness to molt and mate. The male then ushers the female into his den. There, she sheds her shell, and they mate within thirty minutes.

Atema describes lobster mating in romantic terms. He describes the male's tenderness with the vulnerable female, which has a new, soft shell. To copulate with her, he gently rolls her onto her back using his small walking legs. He uses his swimmerets to insert sperm into her body cavity.

After mating, the male sticks around, protecting the female for two or three days. Meanwhile, she keeps his sperm stored in her body until she's ready to produce eggs, which female lobsters do only once every two years. She releases both the eggs (which

This picture shows thousands of fertilized American lobster eggs attached to their mother's body. When the eggs are ready to hatch, the mother will shake her tail, releasing her newborns from their shells.

MORE THAN JUST NECKING

Male giraffes go through a routine called the Flehmen sequence when they're trying to figure out if a female is in estrus. The male giraffe rubs his head against the female's backside until she urinates in his mouth. He can tell by the taste of her urine whether she's in heat. If she is, he'll pursue her, hoping to copulate. But she may stalk away, waiting to see if a more preferable male will approach her.

Meanwhile, to win mating rights, males will wrestle one another with their necks. Usually the one with the longer neck wins the wrestling match—and the female. But female giraffes don't wait for males to do all the courting. If she spots a male she likes, a female will rub her behind against him, trying to get him to Flehmen so she can pee in his mouth. She's more likely to pee in the mouth of an older, more dominant male than in the mouth of a younger one. By choosing a powerful male, she is helping to ensure that she will have strong, healthy babies.

Two male giraffes battle for mating rights by wrestling with their necks. Sometimes male giraffes ignore females and have sex with one another.

Many male giraffes are not focused on females, however. Researchers have found that male giraffes often have same-sex relations. This activity includes rubbing necks together and mounting one another from behind for genital stimulation. Homosexual behavior is not uncommon in the animal kingdom. Male sheep, male and female bonobos, female Japanese macaques, male fruit flies, and female Laysan albatrosses, among other animals, exhibit same-sex sexual behavior.

can number in the thousands) and the stored sperm at the same time. The sperm fertilizes the eggs, which then remain under the mother lobster's tail, attached to her body by a sticky substance. The eggs stay there, incubated by the mother's tail for nine to twelve months. When they are ready to hatch, the mother shakes her tail. The shaking releases the newborns from their eggshells.

A PRICKLY PROPOSAL

On land, if you find a few thousand quills on the forest floor, it's a good sign that porcupines have been playing mating games. Porcupines are heavyset mammals. Their bodies are almost entirely covered with sharp, stiff quills. Old World porcupines (family Hystricidae), found in Europe, Africa, India, and Southeast Asia, mate several times a year. New World porcupines (family Erethizontidae) mate only once a year. New World males that want a shot at mating have to act fast, since females are in estrus for only eight to twelve hours each year.

As she starts to go into estrus, the female porcupine emits pheromones via her vaginal mucus and urine. Male porcupines that pick up this musky message hang around under the tree hollow where the female makes her den. Males will jockey for position under the tree, slapping one another with quilled tails, biting, and wrestling to keep other males away.

The winner—the male that manages to do the most damage to his rivals—hangs out on a branch of the female's tree, guarding her from sexual competitors on the ground. When her scent shows that she is ready to ovulate, or release her eggs, the male sprays urine at her from his erect penis. His urine is full of his own pheromones, and they might cause the female to come into full estrus. But if she doesn't want to mate with that particular male, she'll shake his spray from her body and fight him off by biting or by other aggressive behavior.

If she accepts his advances, she'll turn toward him and lift her tail, revealing her hindquarters, the only part of her body not armored in quills. She'll allow the male to mount her from behind, once, twice, or more over the course of an hour. During copulation, the male deposits sperm into the female's vagina. If the mating is successful, the female will become pregnant and will deliver a baby seven months later. A baby porcupine is called a porcupette.

WHAT A WASTE!

Hippopotamuses use both urine and feces to attract mates. Both male and female hippopotamuses will urinate and defecate at the same time and then spread the waste around by flinging it with their tails. Pheromones in the waste attract the opposite sex for mating.

This hyena is not a male but a female. She both has sex and gives birth through her enlarged clitoris, also called a pseudopenis.

CHAPTER 6
WEIRD EQUIPMENT

Animal mating can involve some pretty exotic genitalia. This equipment includes giant penises and detachable penises that travel from the male to the female on their own. It also includes "love darts" shot by snails during sex. On the female side, equipment includes clitorises long enough to be mistaken for penises, vaginas that can turn aside unwanted sperm, and uteruses (wombs) served by not one but three vaginas.

Some of this equipment can complicate mating. For instance, banana slugs (which are hermaphrodites, with both penises and vaginas) have penises 6 to 8 inches (15 to 20 centimeters) long, almost as long as their entire bodies. For successful mating, a banana slug must choose a partner of the same size.

LUCKY IN LOVE

The males of many mammals, including walruses, hedgehogs, bears, bats, gorillas, and dogs, have baculums, also known as penis bones. This bone is found inside the penis.

A baculum adds stiffness to the penis during sex. Scientists think it may also give sexual pleasure to the female, help the male transmit more sperm, or make the penis seem bigger—which appeals to the females of many species.

Baculums are highly diverse. Two closely related species may have baculums of different sizes and shapes. Some tiny animals have large baculums, and some large animals have tiny ones. Fossil hunters discovered the largest known baculum—4.5 feet (1.4 m) long—in the permafrost (a frozen layer of ground) of northern Siberia, an Arctic region of Russia. Scientists determined that the baculum had belonged to a male walrus whose species went extinct about twelve thousand years ago.

Many fossil hunters collect the baculums, or penis bones, of dead animals. These walrus baculums come from a nineteenth-century collection.

Some people collect the baculums of dead animals. In the southern United States, the baculums of raccoons—nicknamed Texas toothpicks—are considered signs of luck and fertility. Indigenous Alaskans and other Arctic peoples also collect baculums for good luck. In indigenous Alaskan languages, the term *oosik* refers to baculums of walruses, seals, sea lions, and polar bears.

If the partners' sizes are mismatched, the penis of one will get stuck in the vagina of the other during sex. And if this happens, the only solution for the couple is to bite off the stuck penis so that the two can separate.

Wolf pairs can get in a similarly sticky situation. After mating, the male's erect penis and the female's constricted vaginal wall form a bond so tight that the partners can't separate for up to half an hour. During this time, the male will ejaculate (release sperm) several more times. Scientists think that this tight connection helps ensure a successful interaction between eggs and sperm. It also keeps rival males from breaking up the mating couple.

GIRL POWER

Who's the boss? In the mammalian world, it's usually the one with the most testosterone, a hormone associated with male characteristics such as strength and aggression. Among most mammals, males have more testosterone than females. But among spotted hyenas (*Crocuta crocuta*), which live in sub-Saharan Africa, the females have more testosterone. This extra testosterone makes females 25 percent bigger than males and puts them in charge of which hyenas get to mate and when. To even get near a female, a male spotted hyena has to play his cards right, approaching carefully and behaving submissively. If he doesn't, a female might bite and chase him.

The extra testosterone also gives female spotted hyenas an enlarged clitoris that can measure up to 7 inches (18 cm) long. It becomes erect like a male's penis and is sometimes called a pseudopenis. A female spotted hyena has no vagina. She mates and gives birth through a small opening in her clitoris. If a female agrees to sex with a male, he approaches her from behind, and her pseudopenis rolls up "like a shirtsleeve" according to a *National*

Geographic video, creating an entrance for the male's penis.

The pseudopenis isn't ideal for giving birth. In fact, the clitoral birth canal is so narrow that 60 percent of the cubs of a first-time spotted hyena mother will die of suffocation during delivery. The cubs that do make it out alive get a boost from the mother's hormones.

Biologist Kay Holekamp of Michigan State University has studied hyenas in the African nation of Kenya. Holekamp and her team learned that in the most dominant female spotted hyenas, levels of androgen, another male hormone, rise in the last part of pregnancy. Androgen increases aggression. Scientists say that the extra androgen passed on from the mother gives spotted hyena cubs the pushy, macho attitude they need to compete in life. The females grow up to be dominant like their mothers, and the males try to mate more—increasing their chances of successful reproduction.

MARSUPIAL MOMS

Anyone who's ever read *Winnie the Pooh* knows that Kanga keeps Roo in a protective pouch low on her abdomen. Kangaroos are marsupials, a group of animals that also includes koalas, wombats, Tasmanian devils, and opossums. Marsupials are mammals that give birth to extremely underdeveloped babies. Most marsupial moms protect these vulnerable newborns in their pouches until the babies are old enough to care for themselves. The majority of marsupial species live in Australia and on nearby islands. Opossums live in the Americas.

Pouches aren't the only mothering equipment common to marsupials. Female marsupials also have three vaginas. The middle vagina serves as a birth canal, and the two on each side are for mating. In addition, female marsupials have two uteruses. That means that marsupial moms can have two different pregnancies at once, with the embryos in each uterus at different stages of development. When tiny marsupial embryos (less than 1 inch [2.5 cm] long for kangaroos and even smaller for other marsupials) are ready to be born, they make their way down the mother's birth canal and into her pouch. There they feed on mother's milk and grow until they're ready to meet the outside world. The number of babies born to marsupial moms depends on the species. Opossums can give birth to up to twenty-five babies at once, but koalas and kangaroos have one baby at a time.

A joey (baby kangaroo) lives in a pouch on its mother's abdomen for six to eight months. During this time, it grows from a tiny embryo into a fully developed kangaroo.

TOUGH LOVE

Snails (class Gastropoda) are hermaphrodites, so any snail can mate with any other snail. But that's not the only peculiar aspect of snail sex. Among one-third of snail species, the snails grow bony calcium arrows called love darts right before mating. Partners use these darts to stab one another during sex. The whitish darts extend from the snails' necks, behind their eyestalks, which is also where their genitals are located. (The length of the darts varies by species.) The snails copulate face-to-face, and after pinning a partner with a dart, the stabber leaves the dart behind in the partner's flesh and then grows a new one.

Why does a snail stab its partner this way? Kazuki Kimura, a biologist at Tohoku University in Japan, says that the darts carry a mix of hormone-laden mucus to the snail that is stabbed.

Although the darts themselves don't contain sperm, Kimura thinks that the hormones in the mucus help sperm survive longer in the stabbed snail's body. The longer the sperm survive, the more eggs will be fertilized during mating. Snail sex can last more than two hours, and each partner gets stabbed many times during mating. Both will end up impregnated and will lay up to one hundred eggs, which will hatch two to four weeks later.

During sex the Japanese land snail on the left pokes its mating partner with a curved white "love dart." The dart releases hormones into the other snail's body, possibly aiding in fertilization.

STICK-TO-ITIVENESS

Barnacles (class Cirripedia), native to every marine environment worldwide, are also hermaphrodites. These animals are familiar to boat owners, who sometimes have to scrape crusts of barnacles off docks and the bottoms of boats. English naturalist Charles Darwin, famous for describing the theory of evolution in his 1859 book *On the Origin of Species*, studied barnacles in the 1840s and 1850s. He was the first person to note their spectacularly long penises.

Barnacles are crustaceans, shelled animals with jointed legs. They go through several life stages. In the larval stage, barnacles swim and drift in the water. Larval barnacles then grow oval shells and leave the water. They affix themselves to solid objects (such as boats). As adults, barnacles shed their shells and grow hard protective plates. They spend the rest of their lives fixed in place.

Darwin wondered how an animal that was stuck in place could impregnate another animal of the same species. Because barnacles are hermaphrodites, Darwin at first assumed that a barnacle could fertilize itself using its male and female genitalia. But then he observed barnacle mating up close. He noted that rock barnacles, which measure about 0.6 to 3 inches (1.5 to 8 cm) across, have giant penises. He wrote, "The [barnacle's] penis is wonderfully developed . . . when fully extended it must equal between eight and nine times the entire length of the animal!"

The barnacle uses this extraordinary appendage to reach into areas called mantle cavities in the bodies of neighboring barnacles. Sperm from the penis then fertilizes eggs in the mantle cavity. And if no other barnacle is within reach, you guessed it. The barnacle—being a hermaphrodite—can indeed fertilize itself by using its penis to fertilize its own eggs.

GREAT PROPORTIONS

The blue whale has a penis 10 feet (3 m) long—the largest penis of any animal on Earth. But then again, blue whales are the largest animals on Earth. Their bodies can grow to be 100 feet (30 m) long, so a 10-foot penis is not out of proportion for the whale's size.

The male *Platycleis affinis*, a species of katydid, also has large genitals—and the proportions are outsized. The cricket's testicles, which store sperm, account for 14 percent of its body mass. These big testicles come in handy, since the male katydid mates with multiple females during the breeding season, leaving a small amount of sperm with each of his many partners. To place the katydid's proportions in perspective, a human man with a similar body-mass-to-testicle ratio would have testicles weighing 11 pounds (5 kg) each. (The testicles of an average human male weigh only a few ounces.)

Not all species of barnacles reproduce this way. Gooseneck barnacles, which have long muscular stalks attached to the outside of their shells, have much shorter penises. To reproduce, they use a method called spermcasting. They spew sperm from their penises into the water, which carries the sperm to the mantle cavities of nearby barnacles.

SIZE MATTERS

Barnacles have large penises, but male blanket octopuses (*Tremoctopus violaceus*, residents of the Atlantic Ocean and the Mediterranean Sea) have extremely small penises. That's because male blanket octopuses are extremely small. The tiny male blanket octopus is less than 1 inch (2.5 cm) long—at least ten thousand times smaller than the 7-foot-long (2 m) female.

How do the two mate? Like all octopuses, the blanket octopus has eight arms, one of which (called the hectocotylus) serves as a penis. But unlike other octopuses, the male blanket octopus's hectocotylus is detachable. Called a penis tentacle, this arm fills up with sperm and breaks off from the male's body when he encounters a female. On its own, the tentacle swims to the female and crawls into her mantle cavity. The rest of the male octopus dies shortly after his penis tentacle swims away.

The female stores the sperm-filled penis tentacle—sometimes along with sperm-filled tentacles from several other males—inside her mantle cavity until her thousands of eggs are ready to be fertilized. She lays the eggs, pulls the penis tentacles from her body, and squeezes them, releasing the sperm that will fertilize her eggs. "The female blanket octopus will have the male's arm inside her," explained evolutionary biologist Tom Tregenza of the University of Exeter in Great Britain, "and when she comes to need to fertilize her eggs, she can pull that arm out and squirt the sperm over her eggs like squirting soy sauce onto fried rice."

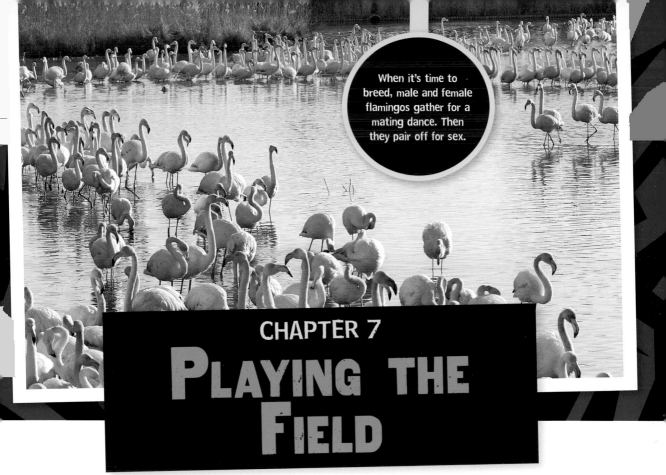

When it's time to breed, male and female flamingos gather for a mating dance. Then they pair off for sex.

CHAPTER 7
PLAYING THE FIELD

When you think about sex, you probably don't think about efficiency. But, in fact, many animal mating strategies rely on efficiency. For example, among certain species, males gather in one place during mating season, in a group called a lek, so that females don't have to roam far in search of a mate. Many bird species gather in leks, as do sea lions, ants, and other animals.

The word *lek* is Swedish for "play." In this kind of play, groups of males stake out territories together to perform courtship displays. In what scientists call classical leks (common with birds), the males are within sight and sound of one another. In exploded leks, the males are farther apart, sometimes out of sight but usually within earshot of one another. Depending on the species, the courtship displays and noises the males make not only attract and impress the female audience, but they also send a "Don't mess with me!" signal to other males. For females, leks make for efficient, one-stop shopping, allowing them to choose from a host of mates—all in one place.

Harems (groups of many females that mate with a single male) are found among many animal species, including elephant seals, sea lions, and some kinds of bats. With many female sexual partners, a male animal has a better chance to continue his genetic line. But within species that have harems, usually only the strongest, largest, and most dominant males get to mate. This way, genes for strength, size, and other desirable attributes are passed to the largest number of offspring. The weaker, smaller, less dominant males sometimes don't get to mate at all.

For animals of both sexes, everybody hooking up in one place at one time—an orgy—can be the most efficient use of reproductive energy. *Orgy* isn't a scientific term, but many scientists use it to describe group mating. During orgies, animals mate with any—and all—of their species that is close by and available, sometimes without concern for whether the partner is ready (in heat), willing, or even able to reproduce. Orgies can look like chaos, but often, they are a very effective mating strategy.

SURROUND SOUND

Among kakapos (*Strigops habroptilus*), flightless parrots native to New Zealand, males form leks in spots with good acoustics—places where sound carries well. The males look for sites where sound can echo off walls of rock or stands of trees. Within a lek, each male kakapo digs his own bowl in the soil, making a depression as big as 4 inches (10 cm) deep and 8 inches (20 cm) across. To attract a mate, the male kakapo stays inside his bowl, where he goes into a sort of trance. His eyes focus inward, glazing over. His chest puffs up, and he booms out a honking, echoing sound that can travel as far as 3 miles (5 km).

The kakapo lek can last for months. Female kakapos don't go looking for leks. Instead, they listen for them. The females are attracted to the male's booming foghorn sound and come out of the bush to meet the males for sex. They will choose a male that impresses them most with his loud booming and puffed-up chest. Usually all the females choose only one male from the lek to father all their chicks.

Kakapos and many other birds don't have penises and vaginas. Instead, they have genital openings called cloacae. During sex a male presses his cloaca against the female's cloaca and sperm moves from the male to the female via these openings.

COME ONE, COME ALL

The male capercaillie, a turkey-like bird native to northern parts of the world, including Finland and Scotland, performs a dramatic display during its lek. He fans his iridescent black tail feathers, arches his neck, and puffs out the feathers at his throat to form a fluffy "beard." He accompanies this display with noisy calls that resemble gurgles, wheezes, and corks popping out of bottles. Some of the sounds are below the range of human hearing, but they travel for miles, calling female capercaillies to the lek to mate. The more dazzling the beard and the more impressive the calls, the more appealing a male will be to a female.

HUMMINGBIRD CHORUS

Hummingbirds (family Trochilidae) are native to the Western Hemisphere and mostly live in tropical regions. Depending on the species and its particular breeding season, hummingbirds form leks that can last up to eight months. For these tiny birds with tiny voices, leks provide an opportunity to sing in chorus, which makes their songs louder and more likely to attract females.

British ornithologist Barbara K. Snow has studied hermit hummingbirds in Guyana, a nation in South America. She notes that during leks, young male hummingbirds hover—wings whirring, songs burbling—in groups called singing assemblies. They include anywhere from a dozen to one hundred birds. Their display includes trading places at perch sites, wagging their tails up and down, mimicking the sex act (with dead leaves), and displaying their gapes—the brightly colored insides of their mouths. Some leks spread over 328 feet (100 m), with male birds perching here and there, singing to attract mates. Each lek has its own song, which females in the area recognize as a mating call. Over the months, juvenile males join the leks and learn the neighborhood song.

LONG LIVE THE QUEEN

Some ants form leks too. Ants live in colonies that may contain hundreds, thousands, or even millions of individuals. These insects recognize a social order, in which the ant queen (a female) is the mother to the colony. Below her in this hierarchy are wingless female worker ants and winged male ants.

Among red harvester ants (*Pogonomyrmex barbatus*), queens have a complex reproductive responsibility. To give birth to the two types of ants that a colony needs, she must have sex at least twice—once with a male that is unrelated to her and once with a male that is related to her. The queen mates with the unrelated male to produce worker ants. These female ants care for the queen; build, clean, and defend the mounds of earth where harvester ants make their homes; gather food; and care for the young of the colony. The queen mates with the related male to produce female ants that will themselves become queens and reproduce. Any male ants produced from this sexual activity serve only to mate with a queen, and they die shortly afterward.

Both queen ants and male ants have wings and can fly. Before mating, the males of a nest fly off and form a lek. They secrete pheromones from glands in their mandibles (jaws). The scent attracts the queen to the lek, where she will mate with at least two males. Scientists think that the queen red harvester ant can distinguish between related and unrelated males in the lek by detecting chemicals called cuticular hydrocarbons, which are different in the two groups. This way, she can be sure to mate with at least one male from each group, although she might mate with more.

During sex, a male ant uses an appendage called a penisvalvae to transfer sperm to the queen's abdomen. The queen stores the sperm in a sac in her abdomen. After mating, the queen's wings drop off, leaving her grounded. She then finds a hole in the ground in which to lay eggs and begin a new nest. For up to twenty years, she will use the sperm stored in her abdomen to fertilize more and more eggs. She will release the sperm, as needed, as the eggs leave her body. In this way, she will produce thousands of worker ants to maintain her colony, a few females that will become queens, and some males to provide sperm to these queens.

BROTHER'S KEEPER

Some animal leks are like "bro" movies—in which two men link up for partying, drinking, and chasing women. Male long-tailed manakins (*Chiroxiphia linearis*), birds that live in the rain forests of Central America, pair up like "bros" to find female manakins. The two males attract female after female with their singing, high stepping, and jumping. However, only the older male gets to mate with the females. He takes center stage, while the other serves as his wingman, or supporting cast.

The same males pair up every mating season to attract

females. The beta male—the younger partner—stays in apprenticeship to the older male for between four and ten years. Eventually, after the alpha (dominant) male dies, the beta male takes over. He becomes the new alpha and gets a new beta.

Biologists from the University of Northern Iowa and the University of Wyoming have studied how male long-tailed manakins pair up. The scientists concluded that the birds choose partners whose songs match their own in frequency (the number of sound wave vibrations over a certain length of time). Over several mating seasons, their songs sync up even more closely. Scientists think that the alpha trains the beta to make his dancing and singing more complex—which attracts more females. When the alpha dies, the other manakin will teach his tricks to his new beta.

SUMMER LOVE

Males aren't the only ones that group together to find mates. Females of many species gather in harems during mating season. California sheephead wrasse (*Semicossyphus pulcher*), fish that live along the rocky Pacific coast of California and Mexico, look for partners all summer long. Their mating season lasts from late June to early September. Females spawn (deposit eggs) as many as eighty times a summer, with a total production of thirty-six thousand to nearly three hundred thousand eggs.

During spawning, which takes place at sundown, females congregate by the dozens in underwater forests of kelp, a kind of seaweed. As the harem gathers, male wrasse jostle for position. Dominant males throw their weight around, shouldering smaller, younger males out of the harem territory, which can be as big as 82 feet (25 m) across.

A male signals his intentions to a female by pressing his bulbous chin onto her head from above. The two swim in a circling dance until the female releases her eggs onto the seafloor. The male then releases his sperm onto the eggs. The most dominant male in the group continues mating until he has mated with every female in the harem—or until the sun sets, whichever comes first.

CAVE-IN

A big animal orgy takes place in springtime at the Narcisse Snake Dens of Manitoba, Canada. The dens host the world's largest gathering of snakes—more than eight thousand red-sided garter snakes (*Thamnophis sirtalis parietalis*). These North American snakes spend their summers in warm marshes aboveground. But during the harsh winter, when temperatures can drop as low as -40°F (-40°C) in Manitoba, they wiggle into fingerlike limestone dens deep underground. They may stay there as long as eight months, avoiding the cold.

In May the snakes emerge from their dens and head toward their summer marsh homes. But before they do, they take time to mate. The males hang around outside the dens in large numbers, forming what scientists call a mating ball. When a female emerges from a den into the mating ball, males immediately mob her. Each one tries to sidle up to her, stretching along her length, signaling his desire to mate by rubbing his chin on her head. That is, if he can get near enough, which isn't easy with dozens

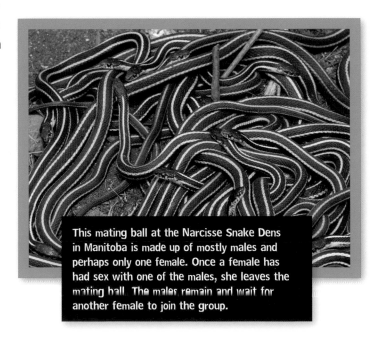

This mating ball at the Narcisse Snake Dens in Manitoba is made up of mostly males and perhaps only one female. Once a female has had sex with one of the males, she leaves the mating ball. The males remain and wait for another female to join the group.

or even hundreds of other males also trying to get close. Once a female chooses a male sex partner, he will insert an organ called a hemipenis into her cloaca and transfer sperm into her body.

Female red-sided garter snakes mate only once with one partner and then leave the mating ball. But the males hang around for four to six weeks, mating with many different females.

After sex, a female will store the male's sperm in her body until she is ready to produce eggs. She'll use the stored sperm to fertilize the eggs. Most snakes lay eggs after fertilization, but red-sided garter snakes are viviparous—their young grow within their bodies and mothers give birth to live baby snakes. A red-sided garter snake mother might have twenty to forty babies at one time.

LOVE CONNECTION

More group sex takes place among sea hares (genus *Aplysia*), which are native to oceans worldwide. These shell-less snails come in various colors. Some have black, ring-shaped spots all over their bodies. Size depends on the species. The smallest sea hares measure just 0.8 inches (2 cm) long, and the longest can measure 27 inches (70 cm). Like most snails, they are hermaphrodites.

Normally, sea hares go about their business in a solitary way. But when it's time to mate, they release pheromones called temptin into the seawater where they live. In Australia, University of Queensland biologist Scott Cummins explains that temptin alerts the hermaphroditic sea hares that their bodies have produced eggs and that sperm is needed to fertilize them.

Sea hares make this fertilization a group effort by linking together in chains of three to twenty animals and mating all at once. The sea hares line up front to back. The snails in the middle of the chain use both their male and female genitalia at the same time. One individual inserts its penis into the genital pouch of the sea hare in front of it while allowing the penis of the sea hare behind into its own genital pouch. The sea hare at the front of the chain will use only its genital pouch, while the sea hare at the back of the chain will use only its penis. At regular intervals, the sea hare at the front will break away and move to the rear of the chain.

This love connection produces hundreds of millions of fertilized eggs at one time. Sea hares lay these eggs in long ribbons that look like spaghetti. They will hatch in ten to twelve days.

SEX ON THE BEACH

By the light of the moon, another orgy takes place during spring and summer along the Southern California coast. There, the water's edge boils with flashing fins and silvery scaled backs bobbing and writhing. This is the running of the grunions, a time when fish called grunions (*Leuresthes tenuis*) get together to spawn.

Grunions spawn for four nights in a row, beginning on the night of a full moon or a new moon. Before each spawning session, the grunion school sends young male scouts to check out the beach. Experts are unsure exactly what the scouts are looking for, but they think it might be the right depth of sand into which females will lay their eggs.

After the scouts return, female grunions swim into the shallows. They dig their tails about 2 inches (5 cm) into the wet sand and release their eggs into the holes made by their tails. Male grunions then release their sperm over the eggs to fertilize them.

After spawning, the force of the ocean waves carries the adult males and females back out to sea. The eggs the females have laid incubate in the sand and hatch about ten days later, sending grunion young by the thousands into the sea.

HOT TO TROT

When it comes to reproductive patterns, topis (*Damaliscus lunatus jimela*), antelopes native to Africa's sub-Saharan grasslands, break the mold. Imagine a lek of ten to twenty male antelopes, each guarding a territory about the size of a baseball diamond. Imagine a stampede of females, not choosing just one male but trying to mate with each of them.

In the animal kingdom, males generally compete for female attention. But female topis are in estrus only one day a year, and they want to make sure they get their eggs fertilized. In the quest to mate, the females become so aggressive that some males run away from them. But most males are willing and able to have a lot of sex. In fact, one researcher observed a single male mating with thirty-six females and collapsing afterward. This example shows that when it comes to sex, animals—like humans—will go to great lengths.

This photo gives a close-up view of a male honeybee's endophallus. Sex between a male honeybee (or drone) and the queen bee ends with the male's testicles exploding, the endophalus ripping away from his abdomen, and his death.

CHAPTER 8
DYING FOR LOVE

For some animals, love comes only once in a lifetime. Scientists refer to these animals as semelparous, which means that they mate or spawn in one season only. They usually die afterward. Semelparous animals include many fish and insects and some invertebrates (animals without backbones). The reproductive strategy of semelparous animals is to expend all their sexual energy at one time to produce the maximum number of offspring.

YOU'RE THE BOMB

Honeybees (*Apis mellifera*) live in colonies of tens of thousands. Many humans keep colonies of bees to raise honey, while other bees live in the wild. Honeybees are found in all but the coldest regions on Earth.

Young drone (male) honeybees have it good for a while. Before they reach maturity, the drones are fed by the hive's thousands of worker bees, which are all females. In addition to caring for the drones, the workers also build hives and forage for flowers, which provide them with pollen for food and with nectar for making honey. The queen of the hive is in charge of laying eggs for the colony.

Some hives have more than one young queen, and these bees will fight for the right to lay eggs. The victorious queen is the one who stings all her female rivals, killing them. With her rivals dead, the queen is ready to mate. She does this just once in her life. She leaves the hive on a nuptial flight, which lasts for several days. She releases pheromones to signal her readiness to mate, and thousands of drones from different hives fly to her.

When the queen selects a drone for sex, the two fly off together, mating as they fly. During mating, the male's testicles explode with a pop as he jams his endophallus into the queen's body, spraying his sperm inside her. The force of the explosion rips the drone's endophallus from his abdomen, and he dies. The queen will mate with between five and seventeen drones in a row during her mating flight. Each one dies in the same sexual explosion.

The drones' sperm don't fertilize the queen's eggs right away. The queen stores sperm in her spermatheca. She will use the sperm for the rest of her life (up to five years), releasing them onto her eggs after she lays them. She'll lay up to one million eggs in her lifetime.

What about the majority of drones that don't get picked to mate with the queen? The worker bees stop feeding them, and they starve to death.

SEX MANIACS

Antechinuses (genus *Antechinus*) also die for love. More specifically, the males of this species have sex until they die. Antechinuses are tiny marsupials. These furry brown ratlike creatures live in high-altitude forests in northeastern Australia.

Every August, male antechinuses begin looking for a female willing to mate. When they hook up with one, the sexual act may go on for as long as twelve hours. The male antechinus doesn't stop there. When he's done with one female, he obsessively hunts for another. After mating with that female, he hunts for yet another, having hours and hours of sex with one partner after another.

During all this sex, the male antechinus doesn't eat or sleep, and the total stress and strain of mating has a fatal effect. The little guy gets infections, his fur falls out, and he may experience internal bleeding. In the end, he collapses and dies. The evolutionary reward of all this sex, although he does not live to experience it, is that his genes are carried on to the next generation.

Female antechinuses may mate with several crazed males in one season. They reserve the sperm in chambers called sperm crypts in their oviducts, the passageways leading to their ovaries. When they ovulate, releasing eggs into their wombs, the sperm saved in their oviducts fertilizes the eggs. Each female produces a litter of four to ten pups.

Ecologist Diana Fisher of the University of Queensland says that the evolutionary strategy works well for the species. The best fathers—the ones with the most strength and stamina—will mate with the most females and will pass on their strength to the next generation. "Females are all [in favor of] this," Fisher told *National Geographic* magazine. "They get the best fathers for their young by mating promiscuously [with many males]."

MAMMA MIA

In the octopus world, it's the mothers that die for love. Most octopus mothers brood, or incubate their eggs, by sitting on them on the seafloor until they hatch. The mothers die shortly afterward. The world record for brooding—held by a deep-sea octopus (*Graneledone boreopacifica*) 4,600 feet (1,400 m) deep in

Mother octopuses incubate their eggs by sitting on them on the seafloor.

Monterey Bay, off the coast of California—is four and a half years.

Biologist Bruce Robison of the Monterey Bay Aquarium Research Institute used a remotely operated submersible to observe this record-setting mother. The underwater vehicle sent a video feed to Robison's mother ship at the surface of the water. Robison first saw the mother hovering over her nest of 160 olive-sized eggs in May 2007. He returned to find her there year after year for almost five years. Before this, the longest brood ever observed was by a captive octopus, which incubated her eggs for fourteen months.

Through the years, Robison and his team watched as their underwater octopus grew thinner and sicklier. Her formerly fleshy purple skin became baggy and pale. The scientists never saw her move away from her eggs to search for food. She was slowly starving to death. Meanwhile, her eggs grew larger. They hatched in September 2011, after which the mother disappeared. She was never seen again.

Such a reproductive strategy is fatal for octopus mothers. But in this case, it ended with 160 baby octopuses. By the time they hatched, they were big enough to swim away from predators and to catch their own prey.

AN UPHILL BATTLE

It's not easy to swim against the current, but every year, groups of Pacific salmon (genus *Oncorhynchus*) do just that. The five main species of Pacific salmon—chinook, chum, coho, pink, and sockeye—begin life in freshwater streams or lakes in North America, Russia, and Japan. After hatching, the young fish make their way downriver and end up in the Pacific Ocean, where they live as adults.

In the ocean, salmon eat squid, small fish, and eels, building up reserves of body fat for warmth and energy. Salmon will need this fuel as adults when they make a tremendous journey—from the ocean back upriver to the freshwater areas where they were born. Here, salmon spawn. It's an exhausting journey that can take several months and cover 2,000 miles (3,200 km). It's also a massive migration, with as many as half a million fish swimming against the current along a single river.

A powerful homing instinct guides Pacific salmon upriver to spawn in the waters where they were born. During the journey upstream, salmon sometimes leap through the air to get past dams and waterfalls.

A NEW HURDLE ON THE RIVER: HOT WATER

As they swim upstream to spawn, salmon encounter many hurdles. Sometimes commercial and sport fishers catch them as they travel upriver. Sometimes water pollution kills them. In the twenty-first century, salmon face yet another obstacle: climate change.

Earth's atmosphere is warming, a phenomenon created by excess heat-trapping carbon dioxide being released into the atmosphere. People around the world burn massive amounts of fossil fuels—crude oil, coal, and natural gas—to heat and light homes and buildings, power vehicles, and run industrial plants. This burning of fossil fuels releases large amounts of carbon dioxide.

The excess carbon dioxide traps heat in Earth's atmosphere, resulting in higher temperatures in both the air and water. In some places, river waters have become too hot for salmon to survive their spawning journeys. For instance, on the Columbia River between Oregon and Washington State, warm water killed more than 250,000 migrating sockeye salmon in 2015 alone.

To help fish survive on the Columbia River, the US National Oceanic and Atmospheric Administration has opened some reservoirs (artificial bodies of water), releasing cooler water into the river. On the Snake River in Idaho, workers at fisheries have rescued thousands of fish, catching them in tanks and trucking them toward cooler waters. Experts hope that these efforts will allow salmon to survive their journey so they can continue to spawn. Otherwise, the fish may become extinct.

The journey is a struggle: the salmon travel against the water's natural flow. They must make their way over waterfalls and dams. To get past these natural and man-made obstacles, they throw themselves out of the water. In the freshwater rivers, there is little food for them, since they primarily eat animals that live in salt water. So salmon rely on their fat reserves for energy as they swim steadily upstream.

How do the salmon know where to go? Scientists explain that salmon have a natural homing instinct that guides them to their spawning grounds. Scientists think that the fish remember the smell of their birthplaces and follow this scent upriver. They might also have a built-in compass, guided by Earth's magnetic field. This compass helps them head in the proper direction to reach their home rivers.

For Pacific salmon, the trip upriver is a once-in-a-lifetime journey. After spawning, Pacific salmon soon die. One species of salmon (*Salmo salar*) lives in the Atlantic Ocean. Unlike Pacific salmon, Atlantic salmon survive the spawning journey, return to the ocean, and spawn several times in a lifetime. Unlike their Pacific cousins, they don't die in the name of love.

Legend says that swans mate for life. Scientists say that swan monogamy is a myth.

CHAPTER 9
YOUR CHEATING HEART

A re animals monogamous—faithful to one sex partner? It depends on what you mean by monogamy. Biologists recognize three types of monogamy in the animal world. In sexual monogamy, an animal has sex with only one partner at a time or with one partner in a single mating season. In social monogamy, pairs form to mate and raise offspring and then move on to other partners. In genetic monogamy, one male fathers all a female's offspring for as long as they both live.

Examples of true genetic monogamy are rare. For instance, swans are said to mate for life. Two swans a-swimming, their long curved necks forming the mirror sides of a heart, are a symbol of marital bliss. But scientists say that the story of swan fidelity is a myth. A study of paternity (fatherhood) in black swans (natives of Australia and New Zealand) found that one in six cygnets (young swans) in a nest were fathered by a male that hadn't fathered the other five. Albatrosses also appear to be faithful to their partners. Males and females form pairs that last for life. Yet scientists have tested the DNA of chicks and parents among one species of albatross—the waved albatross—and found that the mothers had cheated. In one case, one-fourth of the chicks in a mother's nest had been fathered by a male that wasn't her life partner.

According to the blog *Science in Our World: Certainty and Controversy*, only about one out of every 1.25 million animal species is completely monogamous. "Cheaters never prosper," an old saying claims. But sometimes they do. Animals that cheat on their mates might prosper in that they create more offspring, which ensures the continuation of the species. Jeffrey Kluger, the science editor of *Time* magazine explains, "Nature wants one thing, and what it wants are babies. It also wants lots of them and it wants variety [offspring from different parents], because the greater the genetic variety, the greater the likelihood that the babies are going to survive to adulthood and do well."

BEACH BUMS

Males that maintain harems are the most dominant males in a group, and they don't want subordinate (less powerful) males having sex with the group's females. Among southern elephant seals (*Mirounga leonina*), which live in the Southern Ocean surrounding Antarctica, the biggest, most dominant males are called beachmasters. These enormous bulls preside over harems of up to several hundred females during the autumn mating season.

A beachmaster will defend his mating privileges, using loud noises, threatening gestures, and violence to keep other males away from his harem. Weighing more than 8,000 pounds (3,629 kg), the enormous beachmaster can also injure or even kill females (which are only one-quarter of his weight) during mating.

Two elephant sea bulls confront one another on South Georgia Island in the Southern Ocean. The most dominant of the pair will become the beachmaster—the one that mates with the group's females.

Why do the females come to mate with this aggressive bull? Scientists say that each October, southern elephant seal cows (females) follow an instinctive compass to return to the beach where they were born. They come to give birth and then to mate with the beachmaster. By mating with many females, the beachmaster gets many chances to pass on his genes to the next generation.

In the late twentieth century, scientists made a startling discovery about elephant seals that mated on Marion Island in the Southern Ocean. They noted that many of the pregnant female elephant seals arriving on the island hadn't been there the year before. They had gotten pregnant during the previous breeding season—but not by having sex with the beachmaster.

Nico de Bruyn and Marthán Bester, marine mammal ecologists at the University of Pretoria in South Africa, took a closer look at these females, following them for fifteen years. They discovered that rather than swimming to Marion Island to challenge the beachmaster on land, three-fourths of male elephant seals didn't even bother. Instead, they mated with females at sea. That accounted for all the pregnant females that hadn't shown up for the previous breeding season.

On the beach, females have their pups (whether fathered by the beachmaster or another bull) and nurse them. Once the pups no longer need their milk (after about three weeks), the moms mate with the beachmaster and swim away. They will return to the beach to deliver their pups the following year.

CLEVER KATS

Other cheaters can be found among meerkats (*Suricata suricatta*), small mammals that live in the African nations of South Africa, Zimbabwe, Mozambique, and Botswana. As with many species, some male meerkats are dominant and some are subordinate. Subordinate male meerkats can have a hard time finding mates. They often find themselves rejected by females of their own mob (a group of up to fifty animals) or pushed aside by dominant males. Hungry for sex, these males have figured out how to beat the system.

A group of researchers from Liverpool John Moores University in England studied a group of meerkats in Africa's Kalahari Desert for five years. To track the animals, the scientists outfitted

PEER PRESSURE

Black vultures *(above)*, which mate for life, appear to have a social taboo against cheating. They have been known to attack individuals that are seen as wronging their mates by flirting or mating with others. The taboo seems to work. In a genetic study of sixteen black vulture families by University of Minnesota biologist Mark D. Decker and his team, all the chicks in each nest were found to have the same fathers.

some of them with radio collars. They identified others using recognizable haircuts or dye markings. The researchers observed that subordinate males sometimes resorted to "prospecting," moving off to find groups of unrelated females

Meerkat mobs try to enforce rules about sexual behavior. Subordinate males aren't supposed to mate with females, but they often do so on the sly.

for mating. They covered miles of territory at night, mated with female outsiders, and then slunk back to their own groups again.

All this had to be done on the sly. If a prospector tried to mount an outsider female for sex in sight of others in her group, she would reject him with a slap of her paw. But the scientists observed that the female meerkat would later slip away with the outsider male for up to twenty-four hours at a time—long enough to mate.

The research team used DNA testing to match pups with their pops among fifteen groups of meerkats. The researchers found that 20 to 25 percent of pups came from undercover mating games with outsider males.

MUM'S THE WORD

For three years, a team of US and South African ecologists watched nineteen pairs of gelada baboons (*Theropithecus gelada*) have sex in Simien Mountains National Park in Ethiopia, in eastern Africa. The scientists documented 939 within-pair copulations—sex between a harem-holding male and a member of his harem. (Harems numbered up to a dozen females.)

DOG GONE

Among wolves, females lead the pack. In this photo, Canadian timber wolves fight to establish dominance.

In 2014 researchers studying wolves in the mountainous eastern European country of Georgia made a surprising discovery. The studies started when wildlife authorities tried to learn why wolves were becoming more aggressive toward domestic dogs—particularly those guarding sheep—and more aggressive toward the people who lived with the dogs.

To find out what was going on, researchers sampled DNA from wolves, guard dogs, and a few stray dogs. They obtained DNA from wolf scat (feces), wolf pelts from local hunters, blood samples from captured wolves, and hair samples from dogs. The DNA analysis of these samples revealed that 13 percent of wolves in the region had dog lineage and that 10 percent of the dogs were related to wolves. In other words, the dogs and wolves had been mating. The animals born of the dog–wolf pairings were bold and were more likely than full-blooded wolves to approach dogs and people.

Scientists are noting similar cross-species breeding in the United States and elsewhere. As their traditional habitats have been invaded by human development, wolves have moved closer to urban areas. As their habitats have decreased, it has become harder for wolves to find mating partners of their own species. The same is true of coyotes. Both wolves and coyotes are increasingly mating with dogs. Members of the same genus, wolves, coyotes, and dogs are all related and are able to interbreed and produce offspring, although not all related species can do so. Scientists say that cross-species mating helps drive evolution, over time leading to the emergence of entirely new species.

Male gelada baboons normally yell during sex, which made it easy for the researchers to identify baboon mating.

The researchers also observed ninety-three matings between females and subordinate male gelada baboons. These males, because of their subordinate status, were not supposed to be having sex. To keep their mating a secret, the males kept a good physical distance between themselves and the dominant males. They also kept quiet during sex. One of the researchers, Aliza le Roux, refers to such behavior as tactical deception. She describes it as "doing something that's benefiting you—when you are cheating, basically—but you are actively doing something to not be discovered."

Not all the cheaters got away with it. If a dominant male baboon realized that a subordinate male was having sex, he would rush in and bite the offender. That would end that particular mating session. But later, the bitten baboon would try again to mate on the sly. The urge to have sex—to pass on one's genes—is strong, and most animals will go to great lengths for the experience.

Only four northern white rhinos remain on Earth. Scientists hope to use reproductive technologies such as in vitro fertilization to impregnate females and keep the species from dying out completely.

CONCLUSION:
FUTURE STOCK

On a summer day in 2015, Nabire, a female northern white rhinoceros, died in a zoo in the Czech Republic. Thousands of northern white rhinos once roamed eastern and central Africa, but because of human hunting and habitat destruction, the species is near extinction. With Nabire's death, only four northern white rhinos remain on Earth. None of them has ever lived in the wild, and only one is a male. Scientists consider him, at the age of forty-two, to be too old to mate. With Nabire's death, the northern white rhino appears to be on the brink of extinction.

Yet scientists have hope. They believe that southern white rhinoceroses, native to southern Africa and not endangered, might be able to produce offspring with the remaining northern white rhino females, extending the species' genetic line. Scientists don't yet know whether the two species will be able to interbreed successfully, and any offspring that result won't be 100 percent northern white rhino. But scientists say that even a partial northern white rhino would be better than none at all.

To increase the chances of success, scientists are considering reproductive techniques used by humans who have trouble conceiving children. These techniques include in vitro fertilization (IVF). In this process, doctors remove eggs from the mother's ovaries and fertilize them in a laboratory dish using sperm from the father. The resulting embryo is then transplanted into the mother's womb, where it might develop into a fetus and become a healthy baby. Scientists have successfully used IVF to produce litters of puppies and other animals. With luck and similar IVF technology, scientists might be able to save the northern white rhino from extinction.

AN EXTINCTION CRISIS

Even before humans lived on Earth, many plant and animal species went extinct over time. These species were unable to find enough food, evade predators, or reproduce, and their numbers died out completely. This natural process of extinction is called background extinction, and it continues in the modern world. But modern human activities—including air and water pollution; the burning of fossil fuels (leading to climate change); hunting;

Two box jellyfish have sex. Successful animal mating ensures that species continue from one generation to the next.

overfishing; and the destruction of forests, wetlands, and other wildlife habitat—have greatly intensified extinction rates. According to the World Wildlife Fund (WWF), species loss in the twenty-first century is between one thousand and ten thousand times the natural extinction rate. Estimates vary on how many species are represented by this statistic. According to the lowest estimates, Earth is home to about two million species. So based on the WWF numbers, between two hundred and two thousand species go extinct each year. But some estimates put the number of species on Earth as high as one hundred million (a number that includes millions of yet unidentified insects and microbes). That would mean (according to the same WWF numbers) that between ten thousand and one hundred thousand species are lost to extinction each year.

All life on Earth is interconnected. Plants and animals, including humans, depend upon one another in many ways. For example, animals eat plants and other animals. Birds and insects help pollinate plants and spread seeds. Ants and earthworms stir up the soil, keeping it healthy for growing plants. Bats feed on insects that can destroy food crops. So species diversity is key to a healthy planet, and increased rates of extinction threaten life on Earth.

What can we do to slow down this loss? Worldwide, humans are studying animals in all kinds of environments, from the craters of volcanoes to deep-sea hydrothermal vents, from the polar regions to the Amazon rain forest and the Sahara. Scientists are working quickly to identify new species and to learn what conditions they need to survive. The United States and many other nations have passed laws and created programs to protect endangered species and their habitats.

One global program is run by the International Union for Conservation of Nature (IUCN). Using a tally called the IUCN

Red List of Threatened Species, the IUCN tracks endangered animals, determines which ones are at most risk of extinction, and looks for ways to reduce the risk. The largest animal on the Red List is the blue whale. With its numbers already decimated by whaling, this animal is further threatened by water pollution. The smallest mammal on the list (and the smallest known mammal in the world) is the Kitti's hog-nosed bat of Southeast Asia. It faces extinction because people have destroyed the forests where the bat finds its food. The IUCN works with governments and businesses around the world to fight climate change, deforestation, pollution, and other problems that threaten endangered animals. It also supports the establishment of wildlife refuges and environmental protection laws.

At nature preserves, zoos, and research stations, scientists try to breed endangered animals and sometimes return their offspring to the wild. Such programs have helped rescue certain species, but not all animals breed successfully in captivity. This is why many scientists are hopeful about the use of artificial insemination, IVF, and other technologies in saving more species.

Animal sex is part of species survival. In most circumstances, animals mate naturally. If humans are committed to helping rather than hindering them, the great diversity of animals—and life—on Earth will continue for generations to come.

Source Notes

12. Carin Bondar, "The Birds and the Bees Are Just the Beginning," TED video, 9:47, posted March 2014, https://www.ted.com/talks/carin_bondar_the_birds_and_the_bees_are_just_the_beginning/transcript?language=en.

18. "Superb Bird-of-Paradise Psychedelic Smiley Face," Cornell Lab of Ornithology video, 4:30, accessed May 27, 2015, http://www.birdsofparadiseproject.org/content.php?page=83.

19. "Mobula Rays Belly Flop to Attract a Mate," *BBC One* video, 3:01, posted May 13, 2015, https://www.youtube.com/watch?v=oz6zOyZpYTY.

21. "The Peacock Spider—*Maratus volans*," Amazing List, February 26, 2013, http://amazinglist.net/2013/02/the-peacock-spider-maratus-volans/.

24. Venetia S. Briggs, "Call Trait Variation in Morelet's Tree Frog *Agalychnis moreletii*, of Belize," *Herpetologica* 66, no. 3 (September 2010), http://www.hljournals.org/doi/abs/10.1655/HERPETOLOGICA-D-09-00011.1.

28. Christopher Joyce, "Mating Rituals: Male Hammerhead Bats Honk to Woo," *National Public Radio*, last modified June 1, 2009, http://www.npr.org/templates/story/story.php?storyId=101784365.

23. Ralph Vartabedian, "Peckish Woodpeckers Delay Space Shuttle Discovery's Next Mission," *Los Angeles Times*, June 3, 1995, http://articles.latimes.com/1995-06-03/news/mn-8876_1_space-shuttle-program.

49. James Owen, "Watch: Crab Tickles Shellfish for Hours to Find Love," *National Geographic*, May 8, 2015, http://news.nationalgeographic.com/2015/05/150508-crabs-tickle-shellfish-science-animals-new-zealand/.

58. Richard Cox, "The Spotted Hyena's She-Penis," *Curious Cox* (blog), January 11, 2012, https://curiouscox.wordpress.com/2012/01/11/the-spotted-hyenas-she-penis/.

61. Charles Darwin, *A Monograph on the Sub-Class Cirripedia, with Figures of All the Species* (London: Ray Society, 1854), 26.

62. Matt Simon, "Absurd Creature of the Week: The Octopus That's Pretty Much Just a Swimming Blanket," *Wired*, March 20, 2015, http://www.wired.com/2015/03/absurd-creature-week-blanket-octopus/.

75. Brian Handwerk, "Why Some Animals Mate Themselves to Death," *National Geographic*, October 8, 2013, http://news.nationalgeographic.com/news/2013/10/131007-marsupials-mammals-sex-mating-science-animals/.

81. Courtney Hannah Wregget, "The Non Existence of Monogamy," *Science in Our World: Certainty and Controversy* (blog), October 11, 2012, http://www.personal.psu.edu/afr3/blogs/siowfa12/2012/10/monogamous-relationships-in-the-animal-kingdom-do-exist.html.

86. Joseph Castro, "Gelada Baboons Keep Sexual Infidelity Hush-Hush," *Live Science*, February 12, 2013, http://www.livescience.com/27046-gelada-baboons-hide-sexual-infidelity.html.

Glossary

aphrodisiac: a chemical substance produced by an animal that arouses sexual desire in potential mates. An aphrodisiac is a type of pheromone.

artificial insemination: introducing sperm into the reproductive tract of a female animal, using a medical or technical procedure rather than sex. Artificial insemination can bring about pregnancy in animals that have failed to become pregnant through sex.

baculum: a bone inside the penis of certain male mammals, including raccoons, walruses, hedgehogs, bears, bats, gorillas, and dogs. The bone makes the penis stiff to aid in mating.

brooding: laying eggs and incubating, or warming, them (usually by sitting on them) until they hatch. Birds and some other kinds of animals brood their eggs.

copulation: bringing together the genitals (the openings to the reproductive systems) of the male and female of a pair

deoxyribonucleic acid (DNA): a chemical passed down through genes from parents to their offspring. DNA contains the instructions for how an organism will function and reproduce, as well as the characteristics that it will pass on to the next generation.

eggs: reproductive cells produced by female animals and stored in ovaries. When eggs are fertilized by sperm from a male, they develop into offspring.

embryo: an animal in the early stages of development inside a fertilized egg

estrus: in many mammals, a period in which the female's body has produced eggs and she is desirous of sex. The frequency of estrus depends on the species. Estrus is also called heat.

evolution: changes in the characteristics or behaviors of animals over many generations. Animals often evolve as they adapt to environmental changes, competition with other animals, and other outside influences.

extinction: the death of the last member of a species. Animal species go extinct when they are no longer able to find food or to mate successfully. Human activities, such as hunting, pollution, and climate change, have led to the extinction of many species.

fertilization: the chemical change that occurs when a sperm enters an egg, triggering cell division and the development of an embryo

genes: segments or combinations of DNA that parents pass on to their offspring. Genes determine the characteristics of living organisms.

gestation: in mammals, the period of time from the fertilization of an egg until birth. During this period, the embryo develops many of its body systems and structures.

harem: a group of female animals that mate with one dominant male

hermaphrodites: animals that have both male and female sexual organs. Hermaphroditic animals can usually mate with any other member of their species. Some hermaphrodites can self-fertilize, or impregnate themselves.

hormones: chemicals, produced by glands in the body, that dictate the actions of certain cells and organs. Sexual hormones, such as estrogen and testosterone, influence the sexual characteristics and behaviors of animals.

incubation: the process in which birds and some other egg-laying animals keep their eggs warm by sitting on them. During incubation, embryos develop inside eggs, until they hatch.

instinct: unlearned knowledge, inherited from parents, that guides the behavior of animals. Instinct directs animals as they migrate, mate, raise offspring, and carry out other activities.

larvae: certain insects and other animals in their earliest form, right after hatching. Larvae go through several stages before becoming adults. They might change from wormlike animals into winged ones. The different forms depend on the type of animal.

lek: a group of male animals that present a mating display to females in the same time and place every season

marsupial: a mammal that gives birth to extremely underdeveloped offspring. Most marsupial mothers protect their babies in pouches until they are able to care for themselves.

metamorphosis: the process by which animals pass through distinctly different stages of life as they develop to maturity. For example, in its metamorphosis, a butterfly begins life as an egg, develops into a larva, spins a cocoon, and emerges as a fully mature winged insect.

monogamy: a long-term pairing of two animals. In sexual monogamy, an animal has sex with only one partner at a time or one partner in a mating season. In social monogamy, two animals pair up to mate and raise offspring. In genetic monogamy, one male fathers all a female's offspring for as long as they both live.

mutation: a change in the genetic material of an organism, which may or may not be passed on to offspring. Some mutations cause disease, while others make an organism better suited for survival.

natural selection: a process (sometimes called survival of the fittest) in which organisms that are best suited to their environment are most likely to mate and have offspring. Those that are least suited are more prone to extinction. English naturalist Charles Darwin first described this process in the 1850s.

nuptial gift: a present, usually food, that a male animal gives a female as a way to entice her to mate with him

ovulation: the production of an egg by the body of a female animal

parasite: an organism that lives on or in another individual of another species, gaining benefit from the host, such as food or shelter, without benefiting the host in return

paternity: fatherhood. Scientists can test the DNA of male animals and offspring to determine paternity.

pheromones: chemical substances secreted by animals to communicate with other members of their species. Animals that are ready to mate often emit pheromones to let potential mates know they are ready to have sex.

predator: an animal that lives by hunting and eating other animals

prey: an animal that is a food source for other animals

semelparous: reproducing only once in a lifetime

spawning: a period in which female fish and other aquatic creatures lay eggs and males fertilize them. Spawning often involves no physical contact between a male and female.

species: a basic unit of biological classification for plants and animals. Members of the same species have common characteristics that make them different from other life-forms. They are also able to breed with one another.

sperm: reproductive cells produced by male animals. When a sperm fertilizes an egg (a sex cell from a female), the egg develops into an embryo.

spermcasting: spraying sperm into the water, which will carry it to eggs to be fertilized. This reproductive strategy is used by some nonmoving species, such as barnacles and sponges, and may be carried out by either females or males, depending on the species.

survival of the fittest: a process (sometimes called natural selection) in which organisms that are best suited to their environment are most likely to mate and have offspring. Those that are least suited are more prone to extinction. English naturalist Charles Darwin first described this process in the 1850s.

testosterone: a hormone that stimulates the development and activity of male sexual organs

thanatosis: a practice in which animals pretend to be dead to increase their chances of survival. Some animals use the technique to protect themselves from predators that will only eat live prey. Some male spiders use thanatosis as part of a mating ritual.

ultrasonic: falling outside the normal range of human hearing. Bats and other animals are able to produce and hear ultrasonic sounds.

uterus: a body structure in many female animals in which embryos or eggs develop prior to birth

viviparous: giving birth to live young that have developed inside the mother's body

Selected Bibliography

Alcock, John. *Animal Behavior: An Evolutionary Approach*. 10th ed. Sunderland, MA: Sinauer Associates, 2013.

Castro, Joseph. "Gelada Baboons Keep Sexual Infidelity Hush-Hush." *Live Science*, February 12, 2013. http://www.livescience.com/27046-gelada-baboons-hide-sexual-infidelity.html.

Cooper-White, Macrina. "Yes, Mice Can Sing. And You Won't Believe How Much They Sound Like Songbirds." *Huffington Post*. Last modified April 3, 2015. http://www.huffingtonpost.com/2015/04/03/mice-sing-mating_n_6993018.html.

Fairbairn, Daphne. *Odd Couples: Extraordinary Differences between the Sexes in the Animal Kingdom*. Princeton, NJ: Princeton University Press, 2013.

Glover, Timothy D. *Mating Males: An Evolutionary Perspective on Mammalian Reproduction*. New York: Cambridge University Press, 2012.

Hogenboom, Melissa. "European Beavers Pair Up for Life and Never Cheat." *BBC*, February 27, 2015. http://www.bbc.com/earth/story/20150228-beavers-dont-cheat-on-partners.

Höglund, Jacob, and Rauno V. Natalo. *Leks*. Princeton, NJ: Princeton University Press, 1995.

Joyce, Christopher. "Mating Rituals: Male Hammerhead Bats Honk to Woo." *National Public Radio*. Last modified June 1, 2009. http://www.npr.org/templates/story/story.php?storyId=101784365.

Krulwich, Robert. "The Most Unusual Boy Band in the World." National Public Radio. Last modified April 1, 2014. http://www.npr.org/sections/krulwich/2014/03/29/295828844/the-most-unusual-boy-band-in-the-world.

Nuwer, Rachel. "Dogs That Should Be Guarding Sheep Are Mating with Wolves Instead." *Smithsonian.com*, April 16, 2014. http://www.smithsonianmag.com/smart-news/some-dogs-meant-guard-sheep-wolves-are-instead-hybridizing-those-predators-180951122/?no-ist.

Otte, Jean-Pierre. *The Courtship of Sea Creatures*. New York: George Braziller, 2001.

Owen, James. "Watch: Crab Tickles Shellfish for Hours to Find Love." *National Geographic*, May 8, 2015., http://news.nationalgeographic.com/2015/05/150508-crabs-tickle-shellfish-science-animals-new-zealand/.

University of Alberta. "Dinosaur Shook Tail Feathers for Mating Show." *ScienceDaily*, January 4, 2013. http://www.sciencedaily.com/releases/2013/01/130104083114.htm.

Wei-Haas, Maya. "Rare White Rhino Dies, Leaving Only Four Left on the Planet." *National Geographic*, July 29, 2015, http://news.nationalgeographic .com/2015/07/150729-rhinos-death-animals-science-endangered-species/.

Wregget, Courtney Hannah. "The Non Existence of Monogamy." *Science in Our World: Certainty and Controversy* (blog), October 11, 2012. http://www .personal.psu.edu/afr3/blogs/siowfa12/2012/10/monogamous-relationships -in-the-animal-kingdom-do-exist.html.

Yong, Ed. "Why a Little Mammal Has So Much Sex That It Disintegrates." *Not Exactly Rocket Science* (blog), *National Geographic*, October 7, 2013. http:// phenomena.nationalgeographic.com/2013/10/07/why-a-little-mammal-has -so-much-sex-that-it-disintegrates/.

Further Information

Books

Andryszewski, Tricia. *Mass Extinction: Examining the Current Crisis*. Minneapolis: Twenty-First Century Books, 2008.

Bondar, Carin. *The Nature of Sex: The Ins and Outs of Mating in the Animal Kingdom*. London: Weidenfeld and Nicolson, 2015.

———. *Wild Sex: The Science behind Mating in the Animal Kingdom*. New York: Pegasus, 2016.

Brunetta, Leslie, and Catherine L. Craig. *Spider Silk: Evolution and 400 Million Years of Spinning, Waiting, Snagging, and Mating*. New Haven, CT: Yale University Press, 2012.

Ceballos, Gerardo, Anne H. Ehrlich, and Paul R. Ehrlich. *The Annihilation of Nature: Human Extinction of Birds and Mammals*. Baltimore: Johns Hopkins University Press, 2015.

Howard, Jules. *Sex on Earth: A Celebration of Animal Reproduction*. London: Bloomsbury, 2014.

Parry, James. *The Mating Lives of Birds*. Cambridge, MA: MIT Press, 2012.

Schilthuizen, Menno. *Nature's Nether Regions: What the Sex Lives of Bugs, Birds, and Beasts Tell Us about Evolution, Biodiversity, and Ourselves*. New York: Viking, 2014.

Verdolin, Jennifer L. *Wild Connection: What Animal Courtship and Mating Tell Us about Human Relationships*. New York: Prometheus Books, 2014.

West, Krista. *Animal Courtship*. New York: Chelsea House, 2009.

Zuk, Marlene. *Sex on Six Legs: Lesson on Life, Love, and Language from the Insect World*. Boston: Houghton Mifflin Harcourt, 2011.

Videos

Animal sex is well documented in video and film footage. This is a small selection of the many educational materials that are available to learn more about how animals mate.

"The Amazing Barnacle Penis"
PBS video, 2:22.
http://www.pbs.org/wgbh/nova/nature/barnacle-penis.html.
This video from *Nova's Gross Science* series uses animation to show how barnacles mate with their extremely long penises.

"Amazing Video: Inside the World's Largest Gathering of Snakes"

National Geographic video, 3:45.

http://news.nationalgeographic.com/news/2014/06/140626-snakes
-narcisse-animals-mating-sex-animals-world/.

This *National Geographic* video shows the yearly red-sided snake mating ball at the Narcisse Snake Dens of Manitoba, Canada.

"Call of the Wild"

Slate video, 1:00.

http://www.slate.com/articles/video/video/2015/04/male_mice_singing_
mouse_mating_song_recorded_video.html.

This video features mouse mating songs, which have been altered to bring them into human hearing range.

"How Octopuses and Squids Change Color"

Smithsonian National Museum of Natural History videos, 4:37, 3:00.

https://ocean.si.edu/ocean-news/how-octopuses-and-squids-change-color.

Squid, octopuses, and cuttlefish can all change their skin markings and colors to hide from predators, warn rivals, or attract mates. You can see the dramatic changes in these videos from the National Museum of Natural History.

"Mating Moments"

National Geographic Society video, 3:14.

http://video.nationalgeographic.com/video/mammals_african_mating.

This video from *National Geographic* magazine offers a fun look at mating rituals among wildebeests, springboks, and lions.

"Mobula Rays Belly Flop to Attract a Mate"

BBC One video, 3:01.

https://www.youtube.com/watch?v=oz6zOyZpYTY.

This video from the British Broadcasting Corporation shows male mobula rays belly flopping in slow motion, with voice and musical narration.

"Peacock Spider 1"

Live Science video, 6:22.

http://www.livescience.com/39052-peacock-spider-mating-dance.html.

Watch the colorful male peacock spider's energetic mating dance, with narration by biologist, filmmaker, and photographer Jürgen Otto.

"Pufferfish 'Crop Circles'"

BBC video, 2:00.

http://www.bbc.co.uk/programmes/p029nb9g.

In this short video, a male puffer fish crafts a nesting area for his mate.

"Superb Bird-of-Paradise Psychedelic Smiley Face"

Cornell Lab of Ornithology video, 4:30.

http://www.birdsofparadiseproject.org/content.php?page=83.

The mating-dance transformation of a male superb bird-of-paradise from an ordinary-looking bird into a "psychedelic smiley face" has to be seen to be believed. You can see it here.

"What Happens When Animals of Different Species Mate?"
Huffington Post video, 2:14.
http://www.huffingtonpost.com/2014/01/12/interspecies-hook
-up_n_4577872.html.
This fascinating video introduces the wholphin (the offspring of a false killer
whale and a dolphin), the zorse (from a zebra and a horse), the cama (llama
and camel), and the liger (lion and tiger).

"World's Weirdest: Underwater Love Chain"
National Geographic video, 1:37.
http://video.nationalgeographic.com/video/weirdest-sea-hare.
Hermaphoditic sea hares have group sex, linked by their male and female
parts in a mating chain. This *National Geographic* video captures the action.

Websites

Giant Pandas at the Smithsonian's National Zoo
http://nationalzoo.si.edu/animals/giantpandas/
The National Zoo in Washington, DC, is home to four giant pandas (among
them a cub named Bei Bei). This website from the zoo offers a "panda cam,"
panda news, and articles about efforts to breed pandas in captivity and save
them in the wild.

Green Porno
http://www.sundance.tv/series/greenporno
Green Porno, an original series from the Sundance TV channel, hosted
by award-winning actor Isabella Rossellini, explores the fascinating world
of animal mating. The website offers photos, quizzes, interviews, and full
episodes from the educational series.

Jane Goodall Institute
http://www.janegoodall.org
Founded by Jane Goodall, the world-renowned primate scientist, the Jane
Goodall Institute works to protect great apes and other animals, protect
animal habitats and wilderness areas, and improve life for people in poor
nations. The institute's Roots and Shoots program involves thousands of
young people who are working to protect wildlife and strengthen animal
communities.

Wolf Country
http://www.wolfcountry.net
From Little Red Riding Hood to the latest on wolf reproduction, bonding, and
mating, Wolf Country explores wolves in fiction and fact.

World Wildlife Fund (WWF)
http://worldwildlife.org
The WWF works to protect Earth's plants, animals, air, and water. The
website provides detailed information about endangered animal species and
efforts to protect them.

Index

Photo Acknowledgments

The images in this book are used with the permission of: backgrounds: © TabitaZn/Shutterstock.com (white leopard print); © mystel/Shutterstock.com (zebra print, purple leopard print, tiger print); © iStockphoto.com/webstuff, p. 4; © Thomas Marent/Minden Pictures, p. 7; © Buyenlarge/Getty Images, p. 10; © Michael Duncan/Pixoto.com, p. 13; © Laura Westlund/Independent Picture Service, pp. 14, 47; © Martin Willis/Minden Pictures/Corbis, p. 15; © Cornell University/Andrew Leach, Bartels Science Illustration Intern p. 17; © National Geographic Creative/Alamy, p. 18; © Roland Seitre/Minden Pictures, p. 19; © Michael Ready/Visuals Unlimited/Getty Images, p. 22; © Kate Westaway/ Stone Sub/Getty Images, p. 24; © Hugh Maynard/NPL/Minden Pictures, p. 28; © Tui De Roy/Minden Pictures/Corbis, p. 30; © Yoji Okata/Minden Pictures, p. 31; © Mark Moffett/Minden Pictures, p. 32; © Bruno Cavignaux/Minden Pictures, p. 34; © DE ROY, TUI/MINDEN PICTURES/National Geographic Creative/Minden Pictures, p. 37; © National Geographic Creative/Getty Images, p. 39; © Michel Geven/Buiten-Beeld/Alamy, p. 41; © NBCUniversal/Getty Images, p. 42; © Frank Starmer- frank.itlab.us/photo_essays, p. 45; © Segars, Herb/Earth Scenes/ Animals Animals, p. 50; © Tui De Roy/Minden Pictures, p. 52; © Chuck Babbitt/ BabbittPhoto.com/Getty Images, p. 55; © Didier Descouens/Wikimedia Commons (CC BY-SA 4.0), p. 57; © Martin Willis/Minden Pictures, p. 59; © Kazuki Kimura/ (Journal of Experimental Biology) via Copyright Clearance Center, p. 60; © Hemis. fr RM/Getty Images, p. 63; © Jukka Palm/Alamy, p. 69; © Michael L. Smith/ Wikimedia Commons (CC BY-SA 3.0), p. 73; © NOAA/Monterey Bay Aquarium Research Institute/Wikimedia Commons (CC BY 2.0), p. 76; © Jeff Mondragon/ Alamy, p. 77; © Walker and Walker/The Image Bank/Getty Images, p. 80; © Momatiuk - Eastcott/Corbis, p. 82; © Marcel van Kammen/Minden Pictures, p. 83; © Arco Images GmbH/Alamy, p. 84; © imageBROKER/Alamy, p. 85; © Richard Wear/Design Pics/Getty Images, p. 87; © Alvaro E. Migotto, p. 88.

Front cover: © C.O. Mercial/Alamy (monkeys); © TabitaZn/Shutterstock.com (white leopard print); © mystel/Shutterstock.com (zebra print), (purple leopard print).

About the Author

Ann Downer was born in Virginia and spent part of her childhood in the Philippines and Thailand. She worked on many science books when she was a life science editor for Harvard University Press. She is the author of fantasy novels for young readers and several nonfiction science books, including the award-winning YA nonfiction titles *Smart and Spineless: Exploring Invertebrate Intelligence*, *Wild Animal Neighbors: Sharing Our Urban World*, and *Elephant Talk: The Surprising Science of Elephant Communication*.